VISUALITY OF VIOLENCE

In the series *Critical Race, Indigeneity, and Relationality,*
edited by Antonio T. Tiongson Jr., Danika Medak-Saltzman,
Iyko Day, and Shanté Paradigm Smalls

ALSO IN THIS SERIES:

Pacharee Sudhinaraset, *Worlds at the End: Los Angeles, Infrastructure,
and the Apocalyptic Imagination*

Wendi Yamashita, *Carceral Entanglements: Gendered Public Memories of
Japanese American World War II Incarceration*

Joo Ok Kim, *Warring Genealogies: Race, Kinship, and the Korean War*

Maryam S. Griffin, *Vehicles of Decolonization: Public Transit in
the Palestinian West Bank*

Erin Suzuki, *Ocean Passages: Navigating Pacific Islander and
Asian American Literatures*

Quynh Nhu Le, *Unsettled Solidarities: Asian and Indigenous
Cross-Representations in the Américas*

Ofelia Ortiz Cuevas

Visuality of Violence

Witnessing the Policing of Race

TEMPLE UNIVERSITY PRESS
Philadelphia • Rome • Tokyo

TEMPLE UNIVERSITY PRESS
Philadelphia, Pennsylvania 19122
tupress.temple.edu

Library of Congress Cataloging-in-Publication Data

Names: Cuevas, Ofelia Ortiz, 1966– author.
Title: Visuality of violence : witnessing the policing of race / Ofelia
Ortiz Cuevas.
Other titles: Critical race, indigeneity, and relationality.
Description: Philadelphia : Temple University Press, 2025. | Series:
Critical race, indigeneity, and relationality | Includes bibliographical
references and index. | Summary: "Ofelia Ortiz Cuevas contends that the
documentation of racial violence has been an essential element of the
overlapping projects of nation building, imperialism, neoliberalism, and
capitalism in the United States. Cuevas focuses on works featured in
Without Sanctuary (2000) and its exhibition catalog, as well as the
reality TV show COPS (1989–present)"— Provided by publisher.
Identifiers: LCCN 2024053701 (print) | LCCN 2024053702 (ebook) | ISBN
9781439920992 (cloth) | ISBN 9781439921005 (paperback) | ISBN
9781439921012 (pdf)
Subjects: LCSH: Without sanctuary. | Cops (Television program : 1989–) |
Minorities—Violence against—United States. | Police brutality—United
States. | Lynching photography—United States. | Racism—United States.
| Violence in mass media. | United States—Race relations.
Classification: LCC HV6250.4.E75 C84 2025 (print) | LCC HV6250.4.E75
(ebook) | DDC 363.2/320973—dc23/eng/20250226
LC record available at https://lccn.loc.gov/2024053701
LC ebook record available at https://lccn.loc.gov/2024053702

The manufacturer's authorized representative in the EU for product safety is
Temple University Rome, Via di San Sebastianello, 16, 00187 Rome RM, Italy
(https://rome.temple.edu/).
tempress@temple.edu

9 8 7 6 5 4 3 2 1

For my family and the millions not yet uncaged

Contents

Acknowledgments

This book is a long time coming for many reasons and yet maybe right on time. It is a story that unfortunately is a reality for some of us, but belongs to everyone in its need to be known. I am not the first to tell it and I did not do it alone. Here I have the honor to thank and acknowledge the people and places that have been part of this long journey. Anything good about this book is because of them.

First to the public schooling that provided a future that was not intended for me. Thorns and all, I acknowledge the community college and University of California systems, may they continue to belong to the people. In geographical order—north to south and back again—I acknowledge the people who championed and inspired me along the way. I thank Ramon Quezada, Norma Alarcon, Michael Burawoy, David Minkus, Evelyn Nakano Glen, Rachel Moran, Robert Blauner, Mario Barrera, Troy Duster, Michael Omi, Abel Valenzuela, June Jordon, Lonny Ding, Barbara Christensen, David Hernandez, Martin Jay, Harry Edwards, and my homies Sandra Genera, Allison Tintiangco, and Francisca Guzman.

Heading south to San Diego for lessons and guidance, I thank Rosaura Sanchez, Denise Ferreria da Silva, Ross Frank, Charles Briggs, Yen Espiritu, Lisa Lowe, Mike Murashige, Laura Pulido, Quincy Troupe, Jane Rhoades, Wayne Yang, Randy Williams, Long Bui, and Martha Gonzalez, with a special thanks to my cohort Albert Lowe, Lisa Cacho, Ruby Tapia, and Tony Tiongson.

In Los Angeles, the city that I grew to love more than my own home, I thank the people who transformed me and my work: Dylan Rodriguez, Tisa Bryant, Keith Harris, Iyko Day, Cheryl Harris, Saul Sarabia, Deanna Cherry, Robin Kelley, Abel Valenzuela, Laura Pulido, David Lloyd, Ricardo Bracho, Robert Brenner, Romeo Guzman, and David Hernandez.

And finally, back north the Bay Central Valley—a surprise landing—I thank Carlos Francisco Jackson, Kevin Johnson, Raquel Aldana, Carolyn Tomas, Alma Martinez, Wendy Ho, Karen Caplan, Mark Jerng, Suzy Zepeda, Robyn Rodriguez, Ben Olguin, Sharon Knox, Javier Arbona, Erica Kohl, and Jose Arenas. To all my students, I am honored to thank Tina Curiel Allen, Daniel Mendoza, Marlene Mercado, and Robert Echeverria. GO BTS.

And through it all, I thank Horacio Ramirez Roque—in peace and struggle.

VISUALITY OF VIOLENCE

INTRODUCTION

Discipline in the Field of Vision

Scenes of Violence in the Visual Regime

I t was a typical day on the UCLA campus in March 1995. The morning bell chimed loud, and the bright morning sun shined in a picture-perfect blue sky cleared by the Pacific Ocean breeze. Redbrick buildings stood high and solid, impressive in their California antiquity, displaying brass plaques inscribed with Latin verses that spoke of man and knowledge and limitlessness. I crossed the central green, where the perfectly cut grass met the sidewalk pathway with precise angular lines. The large oaks and sycamores shaded thirty or so students sitting with books, papers, and laptop computers. It was a Friday afternoon, and California's brightest youths hurried to classes, meetings, dorm rooms, and parties. As I walked, I noticed a break in the earnest and purposeful movement of the crowd. A police car had stopped in the middle of the narrow campus avenue. I walked in that direction and saw an officer looking down toward the ground. Walking closer, I saw a full-size pickup truck parked in front of the officer's car—dull green and pockmarked with auto primer, with long wood-handled shovels and hoes sticking out above the truck bed. I heard short broken phrases of policespeak on the car radio and saw a young dark Mexican man kneeling on the sidewalk in front of the officer. Another young man was face down on the ground, hands cuffed and legs spread. I stopped to look around to see if anyone else was as caught off guard as I was. Taking a few more steps forward, I was careful to keep myself out of the young man's line of sight. This seemed important—for his safety, for mine, as our acknowledgment of the situation when our eyes connected meant something. His work boots were heavy with mud, and his hands had also been cuffed behind his back. The young man pleaded with the officer in Spanish: "I have a new baby at home . . . please." I looked around for someone to stop, anyone to take notice. I was horrified, ashamed, scared, and panicked, though I am not sure for whom—for the young man, for myself, or for the people walking past. I walked closer. "Can't you just let him up?" I said to the officer. He responded, cuttingly, "Just keep moving."

The young man bowed his head and did not look at me. I tried to catch his eye to let him know that I was there and not leaving. I knew very well that this situation could turn out badly, so I stood, as if my presence would matter, and I watched and waited, witnessing. The young man was pulled hard to his feet by the officer and put in the back of the police car. From there, I knew he would most likely be sent to the Los Angeles County Jail to become part of what was becoming the largest system of incarceration on the planet.[1] The effects on his family and future I knew would likely be devastating. As I turned to leave, there was no one else that had paused to bear witness and take part in this moment that related to us all. I walked back toward the everyday world—bright young students lounging, laughing, hurrying across the quad, heading to classes and events, headed toward their future.

This just-cited story was a snapshot of a day in California in 1995. It was a scene of power and discipline that seemed invisible—a fleeting parenthetical pause in the activities of the campus and the futures being made. The students, faculty, administrators, and other workers moved about as if this unpleasant incident was a part of daily life or as if it were not happening at all. No one looked. They acted as if they did not see. It was both remarkable and disturbing and yet completely insignificant. It is this simultaneous banality and remarkability that is central to understanding what it is that we are seeing when we see police violence.

And, although the scene was not a physically violent or brutal one—nothing for the nightly news, and hardly enough to incite some passing campus activist to object—it was a gross display of power that revealed the relations of force between law and capital and the geographies in which they reside. Moreover, it was a display of spectacular force and power that both manifested and reinforced the visible and invisible forms of state violence and disciplinary practices by which the contours of race, class, and deviancy are defined, cultivated, and deployed. The scene was not an aberration. It was perfectly and tragically normal, then as it is now, and thereby functioned (and still functions) as an example of how the practice of humiliation, violence, and racial discipline in spectacular form contribute to and produce our sense of the everyday. The sight of an officer armed with a gun, baton, and handcuffs represents both the cultural and social standards of law and order, and an officer standing over a young man who is kneeling in subjection or in one's own pool of blood is a common scene of discipline and domination, too often ending in death. The scene of Brown and Black bodies splayed and kneeling on the pavement, one officer resting his hand on the gun in his holster, resembles the past practices of racial violence, which in the West are now condemned and in countries it regards as totalitarian and backward are viewed with indignation. In a nation that espouses the ideals of enlightened democracy, how we live with the violent practices of policing and incarceration that result in the actual death or the suspension of life of predominantly Black, Brown, and poor people demands inquiry. This especially when the nation's incarceration rates exceed those of the developing and third world countries against which the United States frequently takes a moral stand. How, as a nation, have we come to see and then *not see* the extraordinary application of force as somehow common, while also not seeing ourselves as the potential objects of that violence, or, through our complicity at a safe remove, as its authors?

Every evening on television—on the news and on dramatic programs and reality TV—on Facebook, Instagram, and other social media, and on the brick and asphalt streets of our cities, the submitted and violated bodies of Black and Brown people become part of the landscape of state-sanctioned domination and violence. From the video of the Rodney King beating in 1991, which is still fresh in the minds of some of us, to the footage of the bullet-riddled car where thirteen-year-old Devin Brown was shot to death by the Los Angeles Police Department (LAPD) in 2005, Los Angeles, in particular, has been the site of scenes of racial discipline and violence that have made news around the country.[2] And yet, the imagery of police homicidal violence is everywhere. In the years since Rodney King was nearly killed, we have seen/witnessed the brutal murders of George Floyd, Oscar Grant, Tamir Rice, James Boyd, Eric Garner, Richard Ramirez, Antonio Zambrano-Montes, and too many others. That witnessing fueled the Black Lives Matter movement and other movements of resistance against police violence all over the country. Those "fortunate" enough to survive a potentially deadly encounter with police have been injured, some disabled for life, or find themselves imprisoned in what Ruth Gilmore has called the "biggest prison construction programme project in the history of the world."[3] My aim is to depart from the scene at the UCLA campus and survey the wider terrain on which racial discipline and violence are witnessed. This book works to examine the day-to-day practices of managing, controlling, and maintaining populations of the poor and people of color in our contemporary fields of vision or visuality of violence in order to better understand how it is that the most obvious acts of violence go "unseen" or are seen only through the hallucination that those who kill are the victims or that the dead are victims of their own determination.

The incident on the UCLA campus was a visual and material spectacle of discipline, which, in that instance, simply reestablished an already commonly understood scenario of race, violence, and power—the racial body on its knees, handcuffed and bent over the hood of a police car, behind bars, or shot and bleeding on the sidewalks of Los Angeles or anywhere else in the country. At the turn of the twenty-first century, this presentation of the punished racial body is part of the visual terrain of the everyday, both in and on the actual streets of cities and in the realm of representation: in the visual and digital spaces in which we now view them. These spectacles are not so much new as they are resurrected and rearticulated forms of past brutalities that the United States believes itself to have progressed beyond. The visual presentation of disciplined bodies has continuously played a role in the political and economic projects of the United States. These spectacles of racial discipline have been common: the photodocumentation of the massacre at Wounded Knee, the early mug shots documenting Chinese "delinquency" in California, the World War II–era newspaper coverage of the Japanese interned or of zoot-suiters disrobed on the streets of Los Angeles, and the photographs and photo postcards of Southern lynchings are visual objects that hold within them the relation of the racial body to the political and economic terrains of crisis and accumulation—where history is enacted in its material form.

The disciplined bodies, as seen in their visually mediated form, are signifiers of the larger historical practices of racial violence that were once sanctioned, justified, or seen as necessary. These past incidents are now looked upon with acknowledged public remorse and ideals of liberal democratic progress. Yet, racial discipline and violence continue to be a part of the everyday experience as people are increasingly caught up in a state project of unprecedented dimensions—the violent policing and massive incarceration of people of color. At the time of the incident on the UCLA campus, the United States was close to incarcerating two million people; the state had already been at work for ten years building the largest domestic security apparatus of any developed nation. And, although much of this process remained invisible to those not employed by or incarcerated within the prison system, we as a public were (and are now) constantly bearing witness to these developments both on the streets and in our homes.

We can now view with some clarity the most obvious practice of racist state violence in the form of policing not only on the televisions in our homes but also on our computers at our offices or on the phones we hold in our hands. I contend that the contemporary practice of racial discipline in the field of vision—the enforced ordering of race through violent punishment of the body—is similar to past practices of violence and terror that today seem unfathomable and serve more as evidence of the accruement of value in race/

violence. This work considers why the past practices of racial discipline and violence are seen as incomprehensible or reprehensible, while current practices that debase, defile, and dehumanize raced populations continue unquestioned. And, if questioned and brought to the forefront of social and political concerns, in the emergence of organizations such as Black Lives Matter, how and why has police violence not stopped? How and why are police officers rarely charged or indicted for homicide? Now that we *see*, why is it that we still do not know? How and why do some lives not elicit a recognizable ethical crisis?

Since the incident at UCLA, where this project began, there have been moments of police homicidal violence that mark the visual, material, and lived engagement, where as a people and public engage in the viewing and witnessing of racial violence. In 1995, the video recording of the 1991 Rodney King beating by members of the LAPD was still relatively fresh in the minds of the public and was one of the earliest examples of the public visually recording and capturing police violence that was disseminated to the public via news stations across the country. The initial reaction from the public of the beating was one of awe and for a brief moment disbelief. It was clear that much of the viewing public had never seen anything like the raw and unmediated beating King endured while unarmed. However, by the end of the trial, the video documentation of the actual event had become something else— Rodney King had become the threat to police. What we did not know at the time was that we were watching the results of almost ten years of security state build up. On display as well, for those who were looking, were the ideologies required for that building process, one that turned victims into criminals and criminals into victims—a visual hallucination.

Four years before this documentation of violence was turned into evidence of guilt, a mass audience had begun watching a new television show every Saturday night that involved the shooting and violent arrest of poor people of color across the country. Well on its way to making television history as one of the longest-running programs, *COPS* was a televisual documentation of the day-to-day activities of police officers around the country. By embedding camera crews with police units, the program followed the officers during routine patrols in the streets of cities like Chicago, Baton Rouge, El Paso, Sacramento, Tucson, Albuquerque, and Miami. It was a documentation of modern policing and the entry point into the incarceration system. It remains a timeless representation of the detailed practices of violent population management in a time of instability and crisis brought on by the moves and mechanisms of neoliberalism and globalization. *COPS* inaugurated a new era for the genre of "reality" television programming and televisual representation, which was a precursor to the racial violence proliferated on social media platforms. Its creator and producer, John Langly, credited its success to its "unprecedented real-life look at the gritty life on the streets of America."[4] As a hybrid between entertainment and documentary, *COPS* presented its viewers (presumably in real time) the policing of particular economic and political geographies—poor, inner-city, and rural areas across the country—and the police violence used on the bodies that inhabit them.

In *COPS*, we saw predominantly Black, Brown, and always poor people chased, tasered, bitten to shreds by police dogs, humiliated, shot, kicked, and mocked in front of our eyes every Saturday evening at 8:00 P.M. The show presented, in some cases, enactments of pure terror situated in a field of mediated reality that positioned the viewing public as witness to the "crime problem" in the United States. *COPS* became an entity in and of itself, known in a commonsense way to portray the work of policing in the 1990s, when policing was a major tool for building the domestic super security apparatus that came to be known as the prison industrial complex. It is also a visual field in which the viewing public was/is witness to the control of people dehumanized by criminal justice structures. It is an exhibition where we can see the postracial raciality of the criminal non-Human having no ethical value, where the separation of Human and non-Human happens in the labeling of crime and poverty, and not simply because they are victims of police violence.

Eleven years after *COPS* first appeared, the museum exhibition *Without Sanctuary* opened in a small museum in New York, eliciting an overwhelming response from the public of shock and disbelief. A collection of lynching photographs dated between the late 1800s and the mid-1900s, curated by James Allen (owner and collector of the photo postcards), became part of a national discussion on racism, violence, and the ideals of U.S. history, which revealed misconceptions about the practice of lynching as a back road Southern phenomenon occurring at the hands of extremist White supremist groups such as the Ku Klux Klan. What was shocking to the public was the photo-documentation of lynchings attended by thousands (and sometimes tens of thousands) of everyday people in northern and Midwestern city centers and throughout the United States. What also disturbed twenty-first-century viewers of these photos was the level of the violence and brutality and that many of the lynching photographs were turned into postcards and even Valentine's Day cards and sent across the country to family members and friends of the attendees. Images of hung, dismembered, burned, and bullet-ridden bodies of men, women, and children revealed that this brutality was practiced and sanctioned by everyday citizens, people that resembled and were the kinfolk of the viewers of the exhibition in New York in the year 2000. The exhibition was turned into a striking coffee-table photo art book published by Twin Palms Publishers that same year with an introduction by Allen and essays by the writer Hilton Als, the historian John Litwack, and Congressman John Lewis.

Both the exhibition and the book generated a critical and insightful engagement with the twenty-first-century public. And yet, there was a disjunction in this engagement that revealed the way contemporary viewers—the museumgoers, the blog visitors, and the reviewers of the book and museum exhibition—understood their relationship to this violent past. The shock, disbelief, and denial represented in the sequence of recognition—the responses to the exhibition, as well as the book, in the form of blog postings or museum comment journals as well as newspaper and magazine reviews—reveal the liberal understanding of historical progress. It is this understanding of the ideals of law and order, where the construction and accruement of White value establishes itself in the shifting position that is recognized as humanity.

Racial Discipline/Violence and Visual Objects

In this work, both *COPS* and *Without Sanctuary* are visual texts and artifacts that provide a way of understanding the spectacle of racial discipline in the United States and its continued presence in society, in the way we now watch/view homicidal violence enacted by police every day. This book explains how as complex visual objects *COPS* and *Without Sanctuary* are enrolled in the process of sustaining the continuity of racial violence and discipline and the accruement of value in a humanity that is understood only as twenty-first-century White Humanity. The public enlisted by *COPS* gathers in front of television sets across the country to watch the capture, disciplining, and violent containment of those presumed to be threatening and dangerous subjects/suspects. Because *COPS* is presented in a "reality" format—a first for this media form—*COPS* itself functions as a cultural axis on and through which the visuality of race, class, and discipline is formed. Similarly, the postcards of lynched bodies in *Without Sanctuary* powerfully highlight the connection between nineteenth- and twentieth-century legal and extralegal practices of population management through the visual spectacle of fatal (homicidal and genocidal) racial *violence* and socialized racial *discipline*. Although the precise mechanisms through which the criminalized body of color is targeted, displayed, and consumed have changed drastically over the past eighty years, the practice of public racial violence and its ramifications remain remarkably similar in their function: the acumen of the value of humanity as embedded in race and difference.

There is a racial logic to *COPS* as a visual mechanism where the criminal, situated as NonHuman or InHuman and as the antithesis to White Humanity, that is embedded in the social consciousness as a point of departure. As the public is summoned to bear witness, it is already in compliance with the legitimacy and rectitude of the disciplining of the racial body. *Without Sanctuary* and *COPS* both evidence the role that racial violence and the racial body play in the becoming of the United States. This work seeks to explore the reasons the past practice is now seen as shocking while the current practice is considered entertaining. What is at stake materially? And what is gained in these presumed states of visual existence? How do they relate to and play a part in the accumulation of racial value?

COPS is a twenty-first-century visual display of the violent disciplining of transgressive bodies as understood through discourses of criminality—the contemporary legal and popular classifications of juridically defined transgressive behavior. This behavior translates into the material status of a person juridically eradicated, contained, or removed from the social, political and economic landscape. In the show, young Black males presumed to be carjackers are chased down with deadly consequences, "over-reproductive" Latina women have their children ripped from their arms, fathers on parole are humiliated and belittled in front of their families, and Latino males in psychological distress are shot by police officers, the camera focusing in on the bullet hole. The violence registers as necessary and, therefore, erases the life of the person rendered criminal in its entirety, obliterated in the rationality of law, capital, and race.

A little more than ten years after the premier of reality policing, *Without Sanctuary*'s reception indexed the forced historical and racial amnesia necessary to the forgetting and refashioning of a now incomprehensibly brutal practice of racial discipline. Instead of confronting lynching as part of a broad process of racial discipline, replete with historical continuity, it is now managed through a discourse of healing, redemption, and the "lessons of history," revealing a dynamic of recognition that illustrates how the accumulation of "race value" is bound to violence, law, and capital and can transform itself in moments of accruement.

Read together, *COPS* and *Without Sanctuary* illuminate the productive vision of violent spectacle as a practice that consolidates racial difference and productive raciality in complicated ways. This spectacular discipline of the racial body captured in visions of violence symbolically displays the conscious and unconscious enactment of racial order and the maintenance of difference through the allotment of material goods along racial lines. The visions of violence with which we live are signifiers of racial projects that redistribute resources along lines of difference, that identify those who are deserving of the protection of humanity and those who are not. In the practice of disciplining the racial body, the distribution of an intact humanity (in spirit and in body) is the prized resource, at times denied, at others extracted from subjects deemed outside of the law, including those who disrupt it and are, therefore, owed punishment. Thus, the criminalized racial body in the twenty-first century is understood through both its disciplining and the violence enacted upon it. In the twenty-first century, viewing the bodies on display in *Without Sanctuary*, in both the museum exhibition and the photo art book, the viewing public relied on the linear ideal of history and progress as a reprieve from its present relation to racial violence and the accumulation value of White Humanity. It did so through a disavowal and inversion of the violence that appeared so evidently before their eyes.

The viewers of the twenty-first century witnessing identify with only what has become the object of humanity in the field of the museum and the photo art book—the Black, Brown, and Other transgressors hanging from trees. The object of racial violence in the nineteenth and twentieth centuries, at times understood as less than human, becomes, in the discursive field of *Without Sanctuary*, the object of humanist suffering. As this visual and discursive field (book and exhibit) elicit the progressive, humanist, and liberal understanding of Humanity—one of horror and remorse—the focus and disidentification of the spectators and practitioners in the photos is telling. It is here that the whole of the value of humanity sets itself against identifying the inhumanity of its own White relation. The crowds gathered in the twenty-first century resituated their positionality by turning their backs to their own ancestral and material relation to the crowds on the streets of cities all over the United States in the late 1800s and early 1900s. The time passed between the crowds gathered at the lynchings and the crowds gathered in the museums transformed in *idea only* their relation to the racial violence of the past. In the practice of recognition, White Humanity takes the whole of the value of humanity as its own in the twenty-first century and in the suffering of the past object of racial violence.

Here, in *Without Sanctuary*, a linear understanding of history benefits material accumulation in narrative and in body. *COPS*, on the other hand, was and is considered entertainment, set in an ambiguous and untraceable present, unburdened by history, and enjoying a kind of habitual resurrection through syndication that allows it to be dehistoricized and consumed with uncritical enjoyment. This ahistorical placement allows for the similarities of racial violence that can be seen/felt to be set outside the humanist ideals of progression, allowing for a present form of racial violence that can be seen/felt in the present homicidal violence of police today.

This book hinges on mechanisms and themes that enable a material and symbolic analysis of the work of racial violence and discipline. The first mechanism is the concept of racial discipline/violence, which is the exertion of power in force over the racial body, to morally instruct, train, and punish in order to gain control and value. The practice of discipline is seen as necessary to satisfy the commonsense understanding of the racial body as errant, rebellious, raving, and chaotic or as pathologically contagious. It presents a logic of terror and violence against the Black and Brown body and serves as an identifier of the inhuman, transgressive, and criminal. Violence and humiliation are components of racial violence that, even when clandestine, are cultural, political, and economic practices that ensure the efficacy of the state and law, or the symbolic representation of its efficacy. In a particularly visceral and visual way, they inform the relations of race, class, and power in the United States. Even when there is relatively little actual bloodshed, as on COPS, these scenes of racial discipline are typically permeated by the power of the state, by its violence, coercion, and repression, and by its concrete embodiment of the abstract social forces mutually constituted by the visual regimes that emerge from the realm of popular culture itself.

The second mechanism is visuality and the fields of vision: that witnessing, viewing, and watching are foundational to the practice of racial violence and its function in nation making. As the form of what we see and how we get to see changes—from photograph to film and television to computer bits of zeros and ones—the recognition and understanding of the human being and the body also shift. The field of vision is made of the structures that enable meaning and comprehension. In this book, it is the television, the museum, the art book, and the street. It relies on the understanding of the role of seeing in modernity's reliance on the securities of empiricism and the forms of witnessing.

And, finally, history or rather historicity as a device is critical to the book, as it anchors these complex visual objects—Without Sanctuary and COPS—to their conditions of possibility. This project begins with a moment of danger and is marked by several others that reveal history to be a tool and a mechanism that can shift, change, or be used in the hands of the "ruling class."[5] The re-presentation and rewitnessing of lynching in the publication of Without Sanctuary occurred at the same time as a massive racial disciplinary project was being assembled. In this project, history acts as a mirror to itself. In all its brutality, late twentieth-century America was handed this mirror in which, if it wished, it could view itself and the continuity of a spectacular discipline violently enacted on the bodies of the Black, Brown, and poor.

The opportunity provided a cultural site for the present to reckon with its past and its understanding of history, which Walter Benjamin explains is necessary, not so much to recognize "the way it really was . . . but to seize hold of a memory as it flashes up at a moment of danger."[6] The opportunity to establish this genealogy—to seize hold of the memory—was quickly squandered. The moment came and went, with references to its presence lingering only in comparisons with the "modern day lynchings" of James Byrd and Amadou Diallo, moments remembered as homicidal violence that, at the time, were still fresh in memory. Missed in this too-literal analogy were the sanctioned violent disciplinary practices of the police state in the twenty-first century. The shot, maimed, debased, dehumanized, and subjected bodies on *COPS* and the 2.3 million imprisoned persons at the time, the unrecognized subjects of this moment, were eclipsed by the negotiation of reality presented in the pages of *Without Sanctuary*. Very few viewers of *Without Sanctuary* were able to see their own social world or themselves reflected in the images of lynching events hanging on the museum's walls. It is my intention here to prevent that opportunity from slipping away entirely and to look deeply into the pain-filled mirror offered up by history to better understand the present moment of police homicidal violence that we as a public now witness every day.

This work provides an alternative way to understand the work of cultural production and the material practice of racial discipline. Other approaches that examine the form and context of racial stereotypes and the effects of media representations on the criminal justice system too often overlook the material history of crime and race and the role of representations in the projects of race and criminalization as material phenomena. This book places *COPS* and *Without Sanctuary* in relation to each other as part of an excavation of the dense and complex formations of race emerging out of violent legal or extralegal practices and their organizing ideologies. *COPS* and *Without Sanctuary* are not simply flat images in technologically rendered realism; via photograph or video, they are objects that provide an opportunity for a critical indictment of socially sanctioned violence and unchecked state power by calling out the amnesiac way in which we live with and rationalize brutality and violence against raced and poor populations. Chapter 1, "The Visual Regime of Racial Discipline," maps out the provisions for my analysis of *COPS* and *Without Sanctuary*, and the importance of understanding them as complex visual objects that are enlisted in the sustenance and maintenance of racial violence, by providing the theoretical framework for the interpretative work the book undertakes. Chapter 1 also considers work that examines the relationship between race, representation, and disciplinary state systems. Chapter 2, "The Red Record of Material Investment," situates the visuality of racial discipline in *Without Sanctuary* and *COPS* in a longer historical trajectory of the spectacle and genealogy of racial discipline in the United States by focusing on the conditions of possibility from which they emerged and continue to exist. Chapter 3, "*Without Sanctuary*: A Moment of Opportunity," reads *Without Sanctuary* as a visual object at two moments of production—first, at the turn of the twentieth century as it analyzes images of lynching as a testament to the acceptance and celebration of violent racial discipline and its shoring up of white supremacy, and, then, at the moment of the respectacularization of lynching at the turn of the twenty-first century, confronting the ways in which this remediation obscured the contemporary "reality" of racial discipline. Chapter 4, "*COPS*: Racial Discipline at the Turn of the Twenty-First Century," provides a discursive and semiotic reading of *COPS* that illustrates the continued practice of racial discipline. It also explores the role of the program in reestablishing White stability and state legitimacy in the era of late capital.

PART I

1

The Visual Regime of Racial Discipline

Mobilizing Vision and the Racial Body

lthough the experience at UCLA in 1995, which opens this book, was real, the scene had an element of surrealism to it, an odd, out-of-place, and grotesque vision of power, domination, and the impending diminishment of humanity. The Brown kneeling body, head bowed and eyes averted, in the midst of a clear and bright field of vision—the hope and possibility of university education—seemed a dark hallucination. Yet, it was a familiar scene even for those on campus, one informed by both countless mediated images of desperation, pain, and violence in the form of policing, control, and discipline. The visual realms of modern mediation—photography, film, television, and internet—are (and always have been) filled with images of power, domination, pain, anguish, and death. These are the visual narratives of human experience presented to the public through popular culture and now social media. Moreover, they are and have long been everyday stories of race in the United States.

The scene that spring day at UCLA was not a social aberration, even in its surrealism. It was simply an example of the practice of racial discipline and violence that participates in and produces our sense of everyday reality that seemed to have breached the walls of the pristine campus. However, the continuous consumption and witnessing of overt and violent displays of power, domination, discipline, and submission in images, and at times in real-life events, lent those images a quality of everyday normalcy. In addition to the circulation of images of police killings—George Floyd, Oscar Grant, Freddie Gray, and Philando Castile—there were thousands of recorded live-streams of prison interiors, live police chases, and routine traffic stops that began in the mid to late 1990s. This public violence has become its own particular genre.[1] These images testify to the violence of racial discipline in the past and present and illustrate the unrelenting and insatiable appetite the public has for the reality of disciplined and violated bodies. They provide explanations for the social conditions in which they are viewed. Angela Davis explains how the extensive building of prisons that occurred right before our eyes and fundamentally changed the landscape of California happened as images of the criminal justice system became "one of the most important features of our image environment."[2] She explains that, even when we do not choose to watch documentary or dramatic programming, we inevitably visually consume these images to such a degree, that they have become a "key ingredient in our common sense," and that it would take great work to envision a world without them in it.[3]

The scene on the UC campus was part of a larger story in which visuality—how we are able, allowed, forced, and choosing to see and "how we see this seeing or . . . unseeing"—plays a critical role in nation building and material accumulation.[4] As this project addresses the continuity of racial violence and discipline, it relies on the visual as paramount to revealing how the "seeing" logic of visuality is implicated in the violences against the racial subject, which result in the debasement and destruction of the racial body in the service of material accumulation. My reference to the visual, the fundamental principle of perception that enables a reading of images, is an argument that visual images and consumption are central to the cultural makeup of contemporary societies. This chapter examines the ocularcentric way that modern society understands itself and how modernity and culture situate the practice of seeing and looking as paramount to the construction of knowing the world and categorizing and ordering all living beings.

The seeing logic of visuality is situated within the parameters of a field of vision, "a space that is vastly overdetermined" and bound by bodies of thought that produce notions of vision.[5] Irit Rogoff explains the limitations of centralizing vision as a main point of the empirical determination of the world around us, situating seeing (whether as witness or scientist) as a tool of investigation, legitimation, verification, and cognition that has served the Western Enlightenment ideals of truth and science and upheld the Western enlightenment project. In this way, what is seen has legitimacy, as it is "vacated of any political dynamic or role of subjectivity." And the spectacle of discipline, the individual seen cuffed, beaten, hung, or humiliated, is situated in this overdetermined expansive space and is interpreted through the bounded bodies of thought best described as visual regimes. The scenes of violence discussed in this book emerge from a world in which images, sounds, and spatial delineations are inscribed onto and through one another, enabling sometimes shifting layers of meaning and subjective responses to visual media, including television, film, art, magazines, buildings, and even urban environments.[6] Images are no longer simply contained (if they ever were) without question.

This book interrogates images by asking how bodies of understanding are produced through seeing and how particular ideologies are viewed through specific systems and technologies that uphold the needs of institutional subjectivities. Scholars such as Martin Jay, John Berger, and Victor Burgin have argued that we live in an image-driven world where the present moment is defined by the advancing technological media of visuality and where sight is the most fundamental of all human senses. Martin Jay argues throughout his history of the French philosophy of vision that the project of modernity was achieved in large part by the privileging of sight in modern culture.[7] Seeing and sight became the primary medium for communication and the vehicle for the accumulation of social signs and symbols. The ocularcentric character of Western culture that Jay historicizes has sustained the Western Enlightenment project in that to see and observe became a way to control, to know, and to have access to the world. It is a structuring and interaction of a complex and shifting set of visual codes, techniques, and practices historically mobile and varying according to cultural signs. The organizing practices of particular structures exist as regimes of seeing or visual regimes that are productive in making understandings as well as reproducing them. Visual regimes are power-knowledge relations that take various forms and manifest various outcomes.[8]

These regimes are the delineations that tie vision to social power relations, traceable in the institutional matrix of symbolic and material interests that mobilize vision. The power of vision and the discursive work of visuality can be found in colonialism, militarism, capitalism, and law, as well as in male supremacy, as institutional spaces and projects.[9] Institutions, particularly those tied to science and technology or enlightenment and progress are stations of power that mobilize visuality—that is, they see and order the world in often violent ways.[10] Law, in particular, functions through the ideals of criminological/forensic investigation and the practice of trial—the administrative arm of law. Here the administrative practice of law is heavily reliant on evidence and proof—the science of the juridical and the pillars on which it stands the logics of relevance, and evidence in which the visual holds the superior position. The courtroom as well as *Court TV*, the average American living room, coffee shops filled with laptops, a Los Angeles street corner, the cell phone, the visiting room in a detention center, and the viewing room at a museum are all fields of vision delineated by the ideological structures they embody—the systems of law and the state. The way that seeing occurs in each establishes or reinforces a particular vision mobilized through the ideals of legitimacy, deviancy, or transgression.

These mobilizations and orderings through discursive regimes that rely on and legitimate themselves in the practice of seeing and looking are the visual vehicles that have power, through the reliance on and relationship to technology, to actualize themselves. Donna Haraway explains this power in relation to visual regimes and the work of vision: "Vision in this technological feast becomes unregulated gluttony; all perspective gives way into infinitely mobile vision, which no longer seems just mythically about the god-trick of seeing everything from nowhere, but to have put the myth into ordinary practice."[11] The infinitely mobile vision, and its unregulated gluttony, is the universal view of the aforementioned institutional stations shared by those who claim to see with the eye of the universal as a white Western male. It is this eye, with its institutional power, that sees in categories of order. It is also the eye that sees in myths of transgression—the colonial subject, the criminal, the native, and the affected. And, in much the same way that the scientific, male, or colonial gazes have lent themselves to the projects of progress, war, and occupation, the racially disciplined and violated body in the time of crisis is witnessed through the mobilized visual regimes of white neutrality and White Humanity and its (counter) racial logic. The vision of the racially disciplined body is understood through this eye as a particular field of vision, filled with "rational" acts of humiliation, debasement, destruction, and extermination that continue to rely on the discourses of law, science, justice, and technology.

Violence, humiliation, and brutality become part of a rationalized reality as they exist as mechanisms of power. Michael Taussig explains that violence, terror, and chaos in the name of officiality and rationality rely on a process of sense making that necessitates the ideas of truth and reality:

> Killing and torture and sorcery are real as death is real. But why people do these things . . . that is not answerable outside the effects of the real carried through time by people in action. That is why my subject is not the truth . . . not whether facts are real, but what the politics of their interpretation and representation are.[12]

Looking at the social being of Truth and the politics of its representation and interpretation, this question reveals the *epistemic murk* and *fictions of the real* implicated in, as Taussig explains, the violence of colonialism. The fields of vision in which the U.S. modern racial body is disciplined (and destroyed) are delineated by the senses of reality that emerge from structures of legitimation that are *seen*. Photography, video documentation, film, and live streaming video create feeble fictions in the guise of realism and objectivity as they work to flatten out contradiction and the violent chaos of economic projects.

To consider *COPS* and *Without Sanctuary* as objects that are seen through the visual regimes of reality and truth enables this book to inquire how our bearing witness constitutes us as viewers who can live with the everyday brutalities as they occur on our city streets or on Saturday night television. The importance of considering racial discipline through the analytical lens of the visual, and the use of the field of vision, is crucial and not simply because the world has become more reliant and immersed in the constant production of visual information; it is critical to consider the disciplining of the racial body and racial violence through regimes of visuality as an analytical tool in order to read the spectacular display of brutality as a communal performative practice and as a function of the production and material accumulation. Hence, how is it that the shooting of an unarmed and unprotected man is seen as an act of justice and public protection and not the maiming or murder of a human being in the middle of the day on an average city street? Witnessing, seeing, and viewing as acts of collectivity rely on visual regimes, as the eye and its perfunctory function is indicting and implicating larger social relations—what is seen is real, and what is seen is legitimate.

Racial discipline is the spectacular violent work of control and punishment in the form of lynching, beating, shooting, cuffing, ridiculing, threatening, and humiliating in full view of public crowds—those who sit in front of their televisions, visit museums, or gather on the public streets, witnesses who stand in a communal vigil over the practices of spectacular violence in a visual field that determines the value of the performative practice of life extraction. Locations such as city streets, county jail cells, or museums are places that—in relation to the Black or Brown male, female, or child body and the mechanisms used to execute disciplinary practice (police baton, rope, gun, uniform, or white skin)—are symbols, and, when situated in a field of vision, they derive their meaning from seeing in its various modes. In the same way, the museum exhibition and photo art book are illicit and produce a way of seeing that follows a logic of knowledge rooted in enlightenment progress and is situated in the cultural realm of popular television and the heavily patrolled streets of inner-city and poor neighborhoods. The elevated space of the museum and the recognition of its cultural power produce and are part of the production of narrative and history. It establishes and relies not only on empirical accuracy but on the tradition of the earliest human sciences.

Witnessing, surveying, standing vigil, staring, looking, not looking, or, in some cases, hallucinating—a crisis in the certainty of what is visible—are, therefore, engagements of seeing that participate in social constructions that affect the meaning of the spectacle itself. To witness the violent arrest of a young boy on the streets of Los Angeles without question, or to watch with pleasure the shooting of an emotionally distraught man on television, or to view the historical remains of sanctioned violence with the idea that, in that act, a redemptive break with the past is made is to have one's vision fit the ideals of an order that relies on a racial logic.

There is ideological work done in the act of viewing the racial body in a delineated field of vision. Visibility and invisibility take on racial meaning and become the visions of logic and understanding—the regimes of racial discipline that are both realities and illusions as they are mobilized by institutions. Judith Butler aptly calls our attention to the "racist disposition of the visible, which will prepare and achieve its own inverted perceptions under the rubric of 'what is seen.'"[13] She illuminates for us the institutional work that can turn a clear vision of police brutality into a myth of "police vulnerability."[14] These inverted perceptions—in this case, where brutal assailants become the victims—are the visions of racial violence and discipline that become twisted into social hallucinations. Structures such as the courtroom or the police car or the booking station force a perception of justice marked by institutional symbols: the police uniform and badge, the judge's robe, the sanctioned gun are seen within a field of vision of rationality. And yet, they themselves are hallucinations of justice. These twisted or inverted perceptions emerge from a whole constellation of institutional structures situated within the histories of meaning and the meaning and value of the racial body is actualized in moments of material reality. As the lynching postcards were acceptable (in that they were purchased by the thousands and sent through the U.S. postal service), the practitioners and participants of brutal and monstrous murder position themselves as proud purveyors and protectors of justice and order.

Visions and Secrets

Although this book is similar to other works that concern themselves with the relations between state structures, including the punishment system, the police and cultural representation, and how it is that we as a public live with the brutalities of the state, which become common, normalized, but intentionally unseen and unrecognized, this book illuminates the forms of interested power that are hidden in the dark corners of history and inscribed upon the body. It works to reveal that which is veiled behind the curtain of what Benjamin refers to as the secret agreements between the past and the present.[15] The rest of this chapter examines how the meaning and value of the disciplined body can be lost in a humanist understanding of redemption, that is, in facing one's past to change the future.

Much of the work that examines the relationship between representation and the punishment industry has addressed the causes and consequences of racial discrimination in that system as part of the relationship between culture and structure. Scholars of criminology, media studies, and sociology have been contemplating the relationship between media and crime for close to a century. And, although scholars in these fields have examined these relations with fundamental questions ("What makes a criminal?" or "Why/how does media matter?"), they have often done so independently of one another and in the absence of the context in which law is produced.[16] A central point of inquiry in the study of race and crime has, therefore, focused on how racial representations affect people of color, with television and news reporting, in particular, taking up a significant portion of this work. Based on the premise that the purpose of news is to inform the public about the reality of the current moment, the issue of crime reporting has taken center stage, most notably since the Kerner Commission Report in 1968. Often cited as the initial impetus for the study of race and media in the United States, the report claimed that the news media point of view was a myopic white perspective and the foremost cause of stereotypes of people of color as criminals.[17] News coverage has been continuously cited as reflecting and producing the values and norms of mainstream society, with "racial stereotyping" as the center point of news bias.[18] This point of inquiry predominantly focuses on the idea of stereotype as the sign of conflated symbols of exaggerated realities that instigate racist behaviors and practices at personal and structural levels.[19]

As reality television became a more prominent part of viewing crime and the criminal justice system, new scholarship emerged that examined the genre, its effect on viewers, its representation of crime and race, its interpretation by audiences, and its commercial impact on television as an industry.[20] This scholarship considers the social context of this genre as it informs and shapes the nature of institutions, including the criminal justice system.[21] Emerging from the social, cultural, and political world of the neoconservative 1980s, this work argued that this type of programming enabled the era of tough-on-crime laws and racial inequalities in the criminal justice system that emerged during the Reagan-Bush administration. Reality crime programs were informed not simply by the conservative ideologies that supported crime policies but also by the abandonment of rehabilitation and the entrenchment of the get-tough-on-crime stance.[22]

This work rightly questions why the fear of crime remains high, even when the crime rate has actually gone down. Focusing on distorted representations of race, the "reality" depicted is indeed skewed: Black and Latino people are overrepresented as criminals as white people are underrepresented. This is also to say that Black and Brown people are dynamically *criminalized*, while white people are *decriminalized* (they embody a structure of racial *innocence*). They also claim that the "reality" in reality television lends itself to the understanding that criminals in the United States are, in fact, overwhelmingly Black as well as that the disproportionate number of Black people represented as criminals (and White people as police) on television illustrates their point.[23]

The distorted racial representations of crime lead to the "harmful effects" seen in the formation of public policy issues such as the death penalty, sentencing, and prison reform.[24] However, what this work misses and fails to account for is the way that race is signified and materialized through both class and the structure of the state.

Criminology approaches inquiries into race and crime in a similar manner, focusing on whether media images are related to the perceived notions of racial criminality, the policies of overpolicing, or the disproportionate number of Black people incarcerated. Arguing that the assumptions constructed about criminalized Black people (especially males) are due to "entrapment by media imagery," this work asserts that incarceration is integrally related to media representation and that racial discrimination persists in the criminal justice system due to the conflations of the *criminalblackman* as a prevailing repository for the American fear of crime and the contemporary "crime problem."[25] During the early stages of the massive prison building project, O. J. Simpson, Rodney King, Tawana Brawley, Willie Horton, and Mark Fuhrman were each assigned roles in the public perception of reality, which facilitated preconceived notions of the racial makeup of crime in the United States.[26] Stiffer sentences, acts of police brutality, and racial profiling were related to the skewed mediated images and to the racial history of crime in the earliest race laws of the United States, such as the Slave Codes and Black Codes. Kathryn Russell's often cited analysis suggests that these early laws and policies criminalized Black people and that the contemporary problem of the criminalblackman is a legacy of these discriminating laws.[27] Although she rightly traces this historical relation, the limitation of this analysis is the idea that past "discriminating" laws are to be object lessons in how not to structure a racially fair criminal justice system as it existed in the antebellum and post-Reconstruction and Jim Crow eras. The takeaway is that, to run a fair system (and presumably undo history), "fairness principles" should be incorporated to enable the justice system to operate in a racially fair manner.

However, lost in both approaches is the historical functioning of race during that period and the genealogy of punishment as a material project. Criminalizing Black people as well as Native Americans, Asians, and Mexicans worked not simply to maintain a social order of superiority but to manage and handle a social and economic crisis brought on by the shifting status of Black people from unfree to free labor, the occupation and domination of Indian land, and the settlement and occupation of the Southwest after the U.S.-Mexico War.[28] Although both approaches address the role of the media in relation to racial discrimination in the criminal justice system at a time when the number of imprisoned individuals is unprecedented, they overlook the function of racial punishment and its relation to the material interests at stake in the growth of the state and state power at the turn of the twenty-first century.

Here, addressing the "discriminating" structural effects of representations from both perspectives would entail a change in the representations themselves or a change in criminal judicial policies. Within this framework, a more even and fair representation of race would include Black and Latino people as police officers, judges, doctors, lawyers, or professors, and not simply as criminal suspects, to end the prejudice or misjudgment of one group toward another. Their answer is to make these representational changes while, at the same time, enforcing racial discrimination as a criminal practice and developing new criminal laws and policies that would, through the punishment industry itself, create structural change.[29]

These approaches examine the form and context of racial stereotypes and the effects of media representations on the punishment system but overlook the material history of law, race, and punishment even as the persistence of the *criminalblackman* as a narrative continues to corroborate systems of capital.[30] Invoking a prescriptive measure that is to be taken on within the structures of media or in the "criminal justice" system is to rely on the ideals of racial liberalism, which assumes that racism can be expelled from the essential operations on which they, in fact, rely. Racism is instead foundational to the modus operandi of popular culture and mass media and central to the structures of Western law. These representations are not isolated phenomena but regimes that include the very institutions that mobilize our vision. They situate practices of violence in relation to the material reality of modern nation and state building.

In this book the realities of the spectacles of racial discipline and violence are situated within fields of vision that display punitive practices as articulations of power that reproduce new economic relations and designs of social order. I use the idea of visual regimes of racial discipline and violence to understand how violence against the racial body becomes naturalized and understandable through the analytics of law and science. This analysis builds from Ariella Azoulay's explanation of the "civic space of the gaze," a bond of identification between those who are governed and the statelessness of the criminalized subject.[31] The regimes of policing and violence here are social and contractual, creating a field that delineates the manner in which seeing becomes real and seeing becomes witnessing. In her study of looking at and seeing the suffering of Black people through transmediated forms, Courtney Baker identifies the visual encounter as a "collapsing, a falling of the self into the reality of the other."[32] In this way her analysis situates the visual subject in a field of pain that determines not simply the subjectivity of the sufferer but the complex and coconstituting relation of the gaze.

The visual images in the two texts I examine in this book are thus agents and vehicles of meaning that manifest materially in the lives of their respective subjects—both in the past and present and in the past situated in the lived present. There is discursive representational work that can be read in the signs and symbols in the photo documentation of *Without Sanctuary* and *COPS*. However, this book takes on the images as not merely reflective or cause-and-effect agents that inform and entertain; in this book, they are engaged with the viewing public—the witnesses—as real practices that enforce relations of power and enable projects of racial violence through an accruement of racial value. Here visual regimes constitute and produce relations of dominance and racial violence in addition to enforcing and enabling existing forms of power. They suggest the possibility that visuality is capable of doing more than naturalizing and rendering comprehensible racist bodily violence; instead, they catalyze, form, and generate, in a field of raciality and oppressive racial power, a value that is material and protective, both measurable and immeasurable, existing in the spaces between violence and accruement.

This means that, as much as these bodies are representation, they are also a state statistic—a material reality, albeit consumed by viewing audiences, and part of the U.S. system of punishment. When one is watching *COPS*, the reality of the episode is a person being incorporated into the punishment system. They are traceable human beings added to the ever-increasing statistical numbers of imprisoned people around the country who are profiled and understood through the very material statistic they are becoming in the field of vision. So, too, are the bodies hanging from trees and lampposts in *Without Sanctuary*—documented in the photograph, fabricated into postcard form, transported through federal mail, coveted by collectors, and transformed into both gallery and museum exhibitions, where they are counted and named again, and, finally, turned into a photo art coffee-table book—having become the material value of White Humanity.

It is my intention to examine the images in the photo postcards in *Without Sanctuary* and in *COPS* as visual artifacts that are part of a larger visual regime that illuminates the practice of racial discipline and violence as both productive of race and the accumulation of racial value. Although the brutality of lynching is obviously more extreme than the violence on *COPS*, a close reading of the attributes of violence situated in the context of the economic terrain of nation and state building reveals the residuals of past spectacular practices of racial discipline in the real documentation of state violence on *COPS*. The disciplined racial body—hung from a tree limb, in a bloodied and bruised state, stripped of clothing, or beaten and ridiculed by an officer—as a spectacle of hegemonic terror, consumed as banal entertainment, cannot go unexamined in its relation to the history of race and its production. It is, therefore, important to consider *Without Sanctuary* and *COPS* as part of a larger trajectory of the building of social difference through practices of violence and discipline—of hierarchies of race, class, gender, and sexuality—that are produced through *regimes of visuality*. They are not only postcard photos or reality crime drama programming; they are part of the phenomena of institutions and practices of science, law, technology, state policy, and nation building that manipulate the body as the real assurance of social and racial order. And they are images of the destruction of human life, interpreted through regimes that, at once, call for a witness and anticipate a certain type of blindness or myopic view of which life is real and valuable and which life is not.

On Method

To answer how it is that "we" as a people can continually bear witness to and consume with banal affect (or pretend to not see at all) some of the most horrendous displays of racial violence and the debasement of human life, we must consider the complexity (and absurdity and insanity) of a hallucinatory vision that may seem natural. In an attempt to reckon with the violence of modern structures, Avery Gordon explains that "life is complicated," and, by doing so, invites us "to see with portentous clarity into the heart and soul of American life and culture."[33] As she reckons with ghosts left by the violence of the state and the processes of structure, she explains that "social" hauntings—as in the case of the *desaparecidos* of Argentina, the institutionally missing Sabina Spielrein, and the dead/undead Setha—cannot be accounted for "by the bloodless categories, narrow notions of the visible and the empirical, professional standards of indifference, [and] institutional rules of distance and control."[34] The ghosts of the social world (both political and economic) cannot be examined in a conventional sociological manner; their reckoning and true recognition can only come from "a different way of knowing and writing about the social world" itself according to Gordon.[35]

Gordon's theoretical invitation to "see" American society and culture serves as a challenge to examine *COPS* and *Without Sanctuary* as visual texts that hold within them the dark heart and the deadened soul of American culture and the ghosts of those who now occupy the liminal space of incarceration, whose lives have been maimed and irrevocably changed by state violence. Being invited to address and examine the complexity of social life, even a social life that presumes its essence to be the apex of social rationality and science—law and policing, allows for an explanation that may reveal how the violent process of racial discipline contains both a material logic as well as social satisfaction and understanding. The invitation provides and compels an opportunity to not simply "choose a subject (a theme) and gather around it two or three sciences" but rather transgress interdisciplinary boundaries, citing Barthes, to "create a new object that belongs to no one" in order to avoid "disciplining meaning into existence."[36] This theoretical framework for examining the presumably obvious, and yet dangerous, aforementioned questions about the way in which we live within the violent dynamics of racial inequality allows us to see in *COPS* and *Without Sanctuary* the illusion, the unquestionable reality, and the hallucination of the hegemonic logic of the spectacle of racial discipline and the criminalized body.

Within this framework, *COPS* and *Without Sanctuary* are visual objects, productive visions with a complex history embedded in terrors of power, science, technology, violence, and capital. These "visions" cannot simply be understood either by examining the photography in *Without Sanctuary* as belonging to a lost and forgotten history of which we as a nation are ashamed or by studying *COPS* as a television program filled with racist stereotypes or as a contemporary media phenomenon. To examine both as objects in a transdisciplinary manner reckons with the haunting that Gordon tells us is a seething presence, that which appears to not be there. It will attempt to account for the 2.3 million people whose lives are suspended in the state of incarceration, the daily count of the victims of police brutality and police killing, and the ghosts of the 3,500 lynched men, women, and children by explaining how the visual regimes of racial discipline naturalize the ongoing brutality of racial discipline.

The Visual Regime

How, then, does one examine a television program and a set of photographs not simply as a commercial product or museum exhibition but as textual objects that are part of a visual regime? Certainly, to locate and situate *COPS* and *Without Sanctuary* on the continuum of the visual regimes of race, crime, and racial discipline—from the lynching postcards of the South and Bertillon's mug shots to O. J. Simpson's purposely darkened face on the cover of *Time*, the video recording of Rodney King's beating, and the killing of Oscar Grant, Freddie Gray, and Philando Castile—is to first interrogate the ocularcentric history in which the material interest of colonial, imperial, and nation-building projects relied on the visual (i.e., the practices of seeing and of race and difference). The mobilization of vision occurs through the practices of institutions that have assumed an authoritative role in the way we understand visions of violence. In part, the examples in this book demonstrate a forced way of seeing. How we are made to see is the enabling practice and power of ocularcentricity on which *COPS* and *Without Sanctuary* rely: the claim of truth in the "reality" of race seen in a criminal act and it justified consequence, punishment forces an ideal of Humanity as either victim or protector of social good. It is an acknowledgment of the way things really are—seeing is believing.[37]

Both COPS and Without Sanctuary function because what is being seen is perceived to be real and evidential. For COPS, real means enough to assume that crime is truly Black, Brown, and poor, and, in the case of Without Sanctuary, real means enough to be horrified, dumbfounded, and remorseful at the reality of the extreme nature of past practices of racial terror. Both visual objects offer a vision of order, pleasure, redemption, knowledge, and power in the practice of producing racial difference as they rely on the idea of truth in reality. COPS is dependent on the form of ethnographic realism from which it gains its legitimacy.[38] This form allows for an interpretation of crime as something that is committed predominantly by Black and Brown people—a problem presumably so entrenched within this population that the former drug czar and secretary of education William Bennett casually claimed at the height of the drug wars, "If you wanted to reduce crime—you could abort every Black baby in this country and your crime rate would go down."[39] Bennett, for a moment at least, believed this was a rational solution to the problem of crime in the United States. The perception of COPS as real evidence of the nature of crime is likewise understood to be relevant enough to establish laws and policies to control and solve the problem of crime. And yet, as media studies and cultural studies scholars have made clear, this is a skewed version of crime mediated by the editing process and its production as a television program.

On the other hand, and concurrently, the racially disciplined and destroyed bodies in Without Sanctuary are witnessed as evidence of an enlightened civilized society, a social evolution of progressive reform in punishment. The exhibition and book are seen as acknowledgments of the dark past of lynching, which has been overcome and was practiced only by unrecognizable human subjects, or packs of canine-faced mad citizens and monsters, as described by James Allen, the Without Sanctuary author and collector of the photos. The realism of the debased and destroyed bodies in the photos of Without Sanctuary was enough to shake the national consciousness into a moment of reckoning. The prevailing understanding of lynching as a Southern phenomenon of back road vigilantism practiced by hooded and cloaked white supremacists was disrupted by the realism of the very modern settings of communal murder by everyday people across the country. The work to distance oneself from that humanity was quick and swift in order to maintain the value of White Humanity.

There is no denying the reality in each: that there were (and continue to be) real human beings documented in the imagery. However, it is the functioning of reality in the mediated context of "reality television" and in the presentation of real documentation of racial violence in the museum exhibition and book of photography that is the most telling. Reality as an idea is the forced way that we see the spectacle of racial discipline either as real or as social hallucination but always evidentiary. Postmodernist assumptions of mediated reality, the "hallucinatory resemblance of the real with itself," are at work here.[40] In a world that relies on images to understand itself, the idea that all reality is not real until it is mediated is, in part, true, considering the ever-increasing time spent watching television or surfing the internet. The world we walk through is not so much unreal as it is real only in relation to media and its processes of reproduction. However, while considering the racial body in relation to this, one must account for the contemporary experience of living the real *as mediated*. The proposal that all reality is not real until it is mediated dissolves the dichotomy of the signified and the signifier: there is no ultimate signified but simply simulation. But as much as the racially disciplined body is, in its mediated form, part of a shifting system of signifiers—no constant, just continuous simulation—the hyperreal here is not simply in its materialization of an experience in representation but in a corporeal reality that materializes in the moment of state arrest or assault; it is an immediate state statistic, political and economic in form. The disciplined body can now be viewed in its immediate moment in a live internet streaming video of the booking rooms in county jails, which make accessible in continuous real time the violent disciplining and management of Black, Brown, and poor bodies.

Reality here is close to Baudrillard's real—a way to understand the complexity of reality as it mobilizes how the criminalized and disciplined body is understood and, furthermore, *produced* as a component of the visual regimes of race and law. The production itself rests on a history of material relations with seeing and knowledge that hyperreality is dependent on and at moments are the social hallucinations that are accounted for in the disciplined body, it is where the hallucination becomes material actuality in consequence.

The visual regime that appears to us in the form of reality is a construction that is fixed in the project of modernity, where realism, truth, and ocularcentricity lie at the center of the power of the field of vision. Its relation to race emerges from the ideals set forward by early modern European thinkers, as vision and visuality rely heavily on the scientific and philosophical discourses of enlightenment that address vision and what is seen as empirical evidence of the world.[41] Taking this into consideration, the gaze, looking, viewing, seeing or witnessing work as apparatuses of investigation, verification and surveillance enabled by technology. Early forensic practices utilized the photograph to document evidence as the guardian of truth and to document and define the criminal and the insane already instituted in asylums across France and England and their external signs of physiognomic or phrenological degeneration as criminal subjects.[42]

Photographic documentation combined the human sciences and legal ideals of ethics and morality. Science at this time was assigning emotional, psychological, moral, and ethical attributes to the physical visual body. Alphonse Bertillon claimed that through physical evidence one could detect criminality and other character flaws associated with a person's ethnic and racial background.[43] Anthropometry was the first scientific system used by police to identify criminals through photography, which, along with other techniques, differentiated individuals based on their physical characteristics and race. This practice contributed to the prevailing belief that Asians, African Americans, and Southern Europeans were essentially biologically different and inferior to Anglo-Saxons. At the turn of the twentieth century, the human sciences, in particular, tied the legitimation of seeing to the establishment of social control through the documentation, surveillance, and containment of criminals as legal subjects and social deviants, such as the insane and diseased.[44]

Racial difference was, at the turn of the twentieth century, scientific as well as colonial, imperial, and entertaining. Scientific racism, the claim of the biological inferiority of the colonized, became "facts" in the measuring of locomotive ability, skull size, and basic physical being, which were recorded "with precision" by the technology of the camera as it visualized racial difference.[45] Modernity's faith in vision constructed the visual text as critical to knowing the racial subject—seeing, observing, and consuming the images and their display as scientific and ethnographic entertainment. As Haraway explains, seeing race in the documentation of the real is expansive and includes the biodioramas of the Museum of Natural History in New York, where the display of Africa and its inhabitants are set in relation to masculinity and imperial power.[46] The visualities of racial bodies regulated and controlled by the state are more than the rigid applications of the institutions of science, law, and education; they are also commerce and entertainment—the visual image in its modern (and postmodern) state is a source of pleasure, desire, and gratification.[47]

One of the central roles of the modern colonial project was the development of trade with the mission to civilize. "Civilizing the Natives" became the prevailing critical cultural work of colonialism. This colonial visual culture played a significant role in explaining, defining, and justifying the colonial racial order through the study of geography and culture and the mapping out of both space and human behavior. The conventions of anthropology relied heavily on the visual (visual observation and documentation) as a way of having complete understanding and knowing. It was with the ability to see the world through the Western eyes of rationality, reason, order, and meaning that the colonial world could be mastered.[48]

This seeing was legitimated by science, which, while forming racial subjects, naturalized the idea of racial order and the violence that it necessitated. The practice of U.S. racial Othering was forged not only through written text but through visual representations beginning in the late nineteenth century, a time of heightened nation building. Early visual artifacts of racial representation, which gave way to the U.S. *Other* (what became Baudrillard's late twentieth-century simulacra), were used to manage, produce, and maintain racial populations politically, sociologically, ideologically, and scientifically.[49] Furthermore, the visual, colonial, and imperial nation-state building regimes of the 1800s and the early 1900s intersected with the governing beliefs of the scientific documentation of the academy, museums, and colonial/settlement offices.[50] These discourses were as much documentation as they were, at times, spectacular visions of violence and discipline that functioned as modern-day surveillance and as visual products of raced criminality.

The history of spectacle is an integral element of social engagement, theatricality, and the modern activities of crowd entertainment. Spectacles have long functioned as rituals of governance and social control. As the body became an essential component of spectacle, it was also the focus of pleasure and entertainment in the punitive shift from spectacular displays of extralegal practices to the spectacles of modern policing and the invisibility of imprisonment.[51] Foucault's account of spectacle at the threshold of modernity traces the genealogy of the spectacle of punishment from one that was public to one of modern surveillance.[52] The work of public punishment as part of a system of sovereignty (in which the power to take life rested on the grace of the king) relied on torture and physical violence as spectacle. It was a premodern theatric of performance that was a simple exercise and exhibition of power designed to command control of its viewers. According to Foucault, the spectacle of public punishment transformed from the suffering of the body to the suffering of the soul in the modern carceral complex. The spectacle of public executions functioned as the "theatrical representation of pain," which exhibited control through the ability to shock spectators. However, in this Foucauldian context, the spectacle of violent discipline that focused on the body disappeared and reemerged in the form of disciplinary norms in which mass spectatorship became inverted, so the former spectators themselves became objects of the disciplinary spectacle under an invisible, normalizing, and collective gaze. However, while Foucault argued that the spectacle of the disciplined body disappeared behind institutional walls, in the United States, the spectacle of violent racial discipline remains to this day part of the colonial and imperial project of nation building.[53] And it became for a time that which is documented in *Without Sanctuary*—a form of collective enjoyment and entertainment.

Spectacles of violent torture and punishment of Native Americans, Black people in the South, and Mexican people in the Southwest were common in the nineteenth century.[54] These legal and extralegal spectacles of violence and dehumanization continued well into the twentieth century, propelled by U.S. nation-building policies and ideologies. Public spectacles of punishment, legal and extralegal, remained in practice until the 1940s, and, in fact, the last public legal execution by hanging occurred in 1938 in the state of Kentucky. It is, therefore, necessary to consider the bodies that are being or are in danger of being subjected to state violence—the violent manifestations that target raced, classed, and gendered people. The spectacle of the racial body and the forms of violence enacted upon and against it means something particular in the United States, where early colonial and imperial projects of accumulation (i.e., slavery, manifest destiny, and the settling of the Southwest) strewed the geography with bodies as markers of conquest. And, at the turn of the twentieth century, the racial body remained the focal point of suffering as punishment for its transgression and threat to the capitalist project of nation building. In their formative work, *Lynching Photographs*, Dora Apel and Shawn Michelle Smith explain that the photographic imagery of public lynching is obligated to account for time, in the form of history and historical narrative, to gain a truer understanding of what the lynching as a practice of racial violence was at the time it was at its peak—the moments that the photographs were taken—and the moment in which they are rewitnessed. They then become, in a way, another act of lynching, a rewitnessing in another location a short time later carrying a meaning but, in a vessel, incapable of protecting the integrity of the object, so it becomes something else. And, thereafter, in museums at the turn of the century where a rewitnessing occurs and the physics of a geohistorical momentum again transform the object to serve what Benjamin fears most.

Racial Discipline

It is in this way that the racial subjects of *COPS* and *Without Sanctuary* exist as an accumulative entity of capital that reproduces the same instrumentality of the criminalized subjects in the photos of Bertillon and on the scaffolds of Tyburn. However, the bodies of Black and Brown subjects on the realistic ethnographic terrain of *COPS* and in the lynching postcards that hung on the walls of the Roth Gallery in New York in the spring of 2000 are also modern contemporary spectacles—they are, as Debord aptly states, "Capital to such a degree of accumulation that it becomes an image."[55] The spectacle here is not simply a collection of images; it is a social relationship between people, where the main function in society is the concrete manufacture of alienation. The visuality of *COPS* and *Without Sanctuary*—what the disciplined bodies mean as they are read through the form of the spectacle in all of its modes of expression, whether news or propaganda, advertisement or entertainment—reveals that spectacle epitomizes the prevailing model of social life. This means that the spectacle of punishment in the United States was not only racial; it was and is a commodified event and a location for the accumulation of race value through violence.

Neither Foucault nor Debord account for the raciality of the spectacle of the violated and disciplined body and its material relation to the history of colonialism, imperialism, and early U.S. nation building. Foucault nevertheless provides a way of considering sovereign power in the relations of punishment to understand the function of disciplinary spectacle. Likewise, Debord provides a way of understanding the experience of spectacle as contemporary commodity, the *accumulation of mediated images as a consumed product, in this case of the collective* investment in racial discipline. Drawing from both, *Without Sanctuary* and *COPS* are positioned here as sites of mediation where the spectacle, in its formative substance, carries with it the racial and disciplined body in its material and commodified form.[56] The crucial connection between spectacle and commodity is the way that both *COPS* and *Without Sanctuary* are *consumed* as spectacle and, through affect, structure, reality, and reality's social and economic relations, as a practice of becoming witness. Although *COPS* is a media spectacle in the way that media studies approaches spectacle (magazines, advertisements, television sitcoms, dramas, commercials), it is simultaneously documentation of the police at work where real lives are at stake. Therefore *COPS* reality lies in its material relation to the state in the form of prison building, incarceration rates, and death, as each arrest and moment of capture become part of the political economy of the state creating a regime of the juridical.

In this way, the degraded, disparaged, debased, and disciplined bodies are the visual foci of *Without Sanctuary* and *COPS*—symbols and signifiers fraught with social and political meanings that are, in the words of Feldman, branded by the violences that are central to the narratives of the text.[57] Bodies wailing in pain, hanging from tree branches, bent over hoods of police cars, splayed on the ground with arms and legs twisted behind their backs are commodified images as well as material state realities. The branded bodies are the populations that filled the Reconstruction-era landscapes and that now fill the overpoliced poor neighborhoods and prisons throughout the United States: they are bodies rendered as transgressors of presumably normative values and of criminal laws for which they suffer the consequence of racial discipline. In this way, they are a symbolic locus of political and economic processes that construct historical and contemporary racial understandings through an array of visual codes, gesticulations, and articulations.

Bodies in symbolic gesticulations and articulations of transgression incite anxiety, fear, and loathing as they are encoded in the binary extremes of normative middle-class values. Out-of-control sexualities, drug sales and addictions, social infractions, and familial relationships wrought with violence are rendered real in what Stallybrass and White refer to as the *logic of the grotesque*.[58] Using Bakhtinian conceptions of the carnivalesque, these scholars politically frame the ideological repertoires and cultural practices of the high and low social strata to understand the role of the body in society.[59] The body of the low—the grotesque body—is in direct opposition to the bourgeois individuality of the high and represents "impurity, heterogeneity, masking, protuberant, disproportion, clamor, decentered, eccentric arrangements, gaps, orifices, symbolic filth, physical needs, pleasure."[60] Stallybrass and White claim that these gesticulations and articulations of the low incite fear and loathing while generating opposition to what presumably represents the high: censorship of the lower body, closure, elevation (in anticipation of admiration), that which is static and monumental. They claim that the protocols of the body of the high delineate the identity of progressive rationalism itself. In Foucauldian terms, the high represents, on the one hand, the "great age of institutionalization in the form of asylums, hospitals, schools, barracks, prisons," and, on the other hand, philosophy, statecraft, theology, law, and literature as structure and discourse come together.[61] Therefore, the high is a complete embodiment of the rational, ethical, and moral, a righteousness that can be read on the body in its stance, stature, and presentation.

Conversely, the subjects of *COPS* are exposed, soiled, asymmetrical bodies marked by illness and the pathologies assumed to be causes of destitute conditions under which they live and under which they die. These symbolic representations of deviant lifestyles evoke a feeling of urgency, public anxiety, and panic regarding the crime problem in the United States. The presumption that crime originates and proliferates from the neighborhoods, homes, and bodies of the poor justifies the brutalities of policing and incarceration. Yet, what this discursive representation obscures is its own fulfillment of the need to ensure a racial hierarchy that secures capital accumulation.

Accounting for the Immeasurable

In the mediated visuals, public policies, political processes, and state and economic practices, the construction of race and the naturalization of social order often reside in the immeasurable and the unofficial. Feelings of sorrow, anguish, and pain rarely appear in studies of public policy, economics, political science, or popular media. Scholarship rarely accounts for the violent realities of degradation, humiliation, and shame—the various states of dehumanization that are practiced in the physical actions of the state and by everyday people who embody the protected status of White Humanity.

One common practice that is rarely considered in technologies of racial violence is the work of humiliation. As an act or practice, humiliation necessitates that a spectator or a viewer acknowledge, verify, and complete its work. It requires a confirmation of the reestablishment, in this case, of social and human order. Humiliation functions as a social force. It enables the formation of our social recognition of right and wrong, of good and bad, and, in this instance, of race and class. Humiliation frames a set of behaviors for its practitioners and its subjects alike. It is an unofficial aspect of the official training of police officers and other regulatory state agents that is critical in the interactions between officers and citizens. It exists nonetheless outside of the legitimate practices of state control and regulation yet is an accepted norm from which emerges a baseline of banality. In Hannah Arendt's discussion of the forms of power in totalitarian regimes, she claims that systematic domination and oppression are "terribly and terrifyingly normal."[62] Dehumanizing acts, for Arendt, emerge from the volatile practices of bureaucracy and institutions, which render the horrific banal.

Humiliation works not merely as a means of social control at the physical level but also as a mechanism of social feeling that both maintains racial and social inequalities and satisfies the illusion of public order. Raymond Williams's idea of a structure of feeling gives humiliation a tangible dimension, revealing a sphere in which things are "actively lived and felt."[63] Williams asserts that a structure of feeling defines "a social experience that is still in process, often indeed not recognized as social but taken to be private, idiosyncratic, and even isolating."[64] The concept of a structure of feeling takes into account the emotive and unofficial dynamics of the practices of humiliation and renders them real, active, and traceable in state and public practices. The practice of humiliation, as an overwhelming motif in all documented practices of racial violence provides insight into the power and assumed positioning of those who can bestow the entitlement and value of a secured and whole humanity and those who cannot.

In the many times that I have thought back to that scene at UCLA—and recalled the initial feelings of fear, revulsion, heartache, powerlessness, indignation, and anger—I remember most the young man's refusal to look up and acknowledge my presence as I tried to call attention to what for me was an atrocity. I did not have a cell phone then (most people did not), and I had only my eyes and the presence of my body to stand and witness. I looked at him and then to the officers to let both know that my pause and presence, in the day-to-day movement of the campus, meant that I was there to bear witness—that the young man and myself mattered. In that exchange of glances, I was holding the uniformed officers accountable. I knew it as well as they did. The young man's downward glance meant that he knew it as well, and that a demand for accountability publicly could endanger the both of us. I wanted the other students to stop and acknowledge, to recognize what I saw as a dangerous injustice. A collective witnessing may have provided the only way no one would be harmed. As I went on my way at the order of the officer, reluctantly glancing back over my shoulder, the young man—with his head down (out of shame or fear I will never know)—was eventually taken away in a familiar scenario. It was a moment only recorded in my memory but that unrecorded moment was part of a long and violent record of racial discipline and the material investment in upholding the dangerous ideals of Western and White Humanity.

2

THE RED RECORD OF MATERIAL
INVESTMENT

Racial Discipline in the Mirror of History

In the middle of March 2002, I watched twenty-five young men, including my brother, attend a sentencing hearing in Los Angeles, California. That day, these men—eleven Mexican and/or Chicano, twelve Black, one White, and one Asian, all facing various nonviolent possession of drug-related charges—were sentenced cumulatively to 185 years behind bars. That very week, in a *New York Times* article, the United States had been declared the nation with the largest number of people behind bars in the history of the world. I left the building only to see a woman I recognized from the courtroom on her knees, wailing in pain. She had just received news that her son—the brother of a young man just sentenced to three years—had died earlier that morning in Pelican Bay State Prison. That day it seemed moments of danger were everywhere. And for some, they were.

In a matter of just twenty years, the United States had instituted what some prison scholars call the largest state project of the twentieth century: incorporating into its punishment system more than seven million people.[1] Now more than two decades into the new millennium, there are two million people behind bars, with the remainder in various stages of parole or probation. The number of prisons built to house those behind bars grew by 350 percent from 1986 to 1996, including state and federal structures that hold more than twenty thousand people in supermax facilities, as well as thirty-four hundred on death row, including the highest number of juveniles sentenced to death in the world.[2] And the racial makeup of these numbers is grave, as Black men, who make up just 9 percent of the general population, account for 35 percent of the imprisoned population. Over that same twenty-year period, the United States has come under the scrutiny of international human rights organizations for the use of excessive and deadly force by police officers.[3] At the time of the aforementioned scene at the California courthouse, 150 people had been killed by law enforcement officers in New Jersey and New York alone since September 11, 2001. In that same period, Gus Rugley, a twenty-one-year-old Black man was shot more than one hundred times by San Francisco police officers after a high-speed chase; Cau Bich Tran, a twenty-five-year-old Vietnamese woman, was shot by police in San Jose when they mistook her vegetable peeler for a gun; and Nathaniel Jones was beaten to death with a metal baton after being taken into custody by Cincinnati police for shoplifting. Until the killing of Michael Brown and the uprising in Ferguson, Missouri, any state or federal accounting of police homicide was virtually nonexistent. The list of these abuses is extensive but not exact because the wrongful use of force is indiscernible and at times indistinguishable from what is considered standard operating procedure. Although these moments of violence during this period were not as visible to the general public (as they are now when they appear on the internet almost daily), they show that racial state violence at the hands of police was and is everywhere.[4]

At that time, we were already as a public watching police violence every Saturday night at 8:00 P.M. in our own homes as entertainment. At the time that *COPS* was making its own history in its thirteenth year on the air, reality crime shows had gone global: *Placas* in Mexico City, *The Force* in Australia, *Nyom Nelkul* in Hungary, and *Police Camera Action* in the United Kingdom. The visibility of policing in "real time" is, in a sense, everywhere. On the internet, the newly designed medium of live streaming video made it possible for jails to post in real time the booking and jailing of men and women across the country, which in Maricopa County included streaming videos of fingerprinting as well as the initial strip searches of suspects. In addition, the creator and producer of *COPS* debuted a half-hour reality program during the 2007 fall television season of FOX called *JAIL*, which documented the proceedings subsequent to arrest—holding and booking—and is still on the air. I argue that what we are watching on these programs are not simply racist representations of crime and policing but public spaces where we as a public would actually bear witness to the largest prison building project in the history of the world.

The United States witnessed this kind of dramatic and volatile shift in imprisonment en masse once before, following the era of Reconstruction.[5] It was in that era and into the turn of the nineteenth century that the dramatic growth in individuals relegated to the punishment system was so vast that W.E.B. Du Bois was moved to exclaim, "In no other part of the modern world has there been so open and conscious a traffic in crime for deliberate social degradation and private profit as in the South."[6] Du Bois was acknowledging the systematic rearticulation of an economic system that rested upon methods of labor extraction from unfree labor and upon which the rebuilding of the South depended, a system that existed under the guise of a legitimate criminal justice system. He was, in part, referring to the laws that regulated slavery and were immediately readdressed to manage the crisis brought on by the newly freed population of Black people in the South. This reanimated labor, which first took the form of the convict lease system and later of the chain gang, could by the turn of the century be seen in the long rows of men chained to one another along railroad lines or along new public roads. Working long hours under threat of the "whipping boss," the convicts—visible signifiers of reestablished order—were evidence of the institutionalization of brutality. Violence, according to Matthew Mancini, was not grafted onto a particular system of penal management—the system of convict lease was "maintained, at least in part as an institutional outlet for violence."[7] Mancini's claim that the violence was primary in the practice of convict lease establishes the necessity of the extermination of both body and soul in the restoration of racial order tied to labor.

During this same period, the violence enacted against the Black body had reached an apex of spectacular disciplining, which Ida B. Wells accounted for in her work on lynching in the United States. In *Red Record: Mob Rule in New Orleans*, she detailed the executions of Black people by public mobs.[8] As part of her campaign against lynching, Wells documented the violent public deaths of Calvin Thomas in Georgia, who was accused of assault, Charles T. Miller in Kentucky for alleged rape, Isaac Lincoln in South Carolina for insulting a white person, Andy Blount for suspicion of rape in Tennessee, and an "Unknown Negro" for self-defense in Kentucky.

Wells listed the number of lynchings for each of the Southern states and included detailed descriptions of the mob and the activities of the spectators, who came, as she stated, "in crowds of thousands, from cities all over the South with some who watched calmly while others cheered and clapped."[9] Wells accounted for the men, women, and children who were caught up in the frenzy of the event and took away body parts, fingers, hair, and the charred remains of the people burned as well as pieces of the hangman's noose. She explained that the teeth, hair, and fingers of Lee Walker, in Georgia, were taken from his burned body and described an "Unknown Negro," also in Georgia, who was run down, dragged through town by a rope, hung, and left for townspeople to shoot. Quoting an eyewitness to the burning of Henry Smith (a Black man charged with the murder of a four-year-old white girl), Wells wrote, "Even at the stake, children of both sexes and colors gathered in groups. . . . The children became as frantic as the grown people. . . . Little faces distorted with passion and the bloodshot eyes of the cruel parent watched with glee the burning body of Smith."[10] According to Wells, ten thousand people watched the hanging and burning of Smith. His body became the focal point for the anxiety, fear, desire, and loathing of White Americans and the invested interest in the protection of their lives through the ideals of law and order.

While I am not suggesting that the bodies and lives of only people of color have been subject to exacting brutalization in the period following Reconstruction and the era now known as mass incarceration, we must question these spikes in racial discipline and at their timing—What is common to these moments? What crises elicited these particular performative practices of American brutality? The question is twofold: (1) What conditions the emergence of this violence into the collective public sphere? (2) What representational tools, both material and ideological, are marshaled to the task of rendering the spectacular everyday, mundane, and acceptable? But first, we might ask to what end we ask these questions—why does it make sense to draw these connections?

The point of resurrecting this history is not to argue that present-day imprisonment or policing are simple replications of slavery or the brutal acquisition of land but to suggest that the contemporary era of mass prison building and policing, and the fields of vision through which we as a public bear witness to it, are recognizable, to borrow Benjamin's phrase, as a "moment of danger." In Benjamin's transfixing contemplation of history, he compels us to recognize the past:

> The past carries with it a temporal index by which it is referred to redemption. There is a secret agreement between past generations and the present one. . . . As flowers turn toward the sun, by dint of a secret heliotropism the past strives to turn toward that sun which is rising in the sky of history. A historical materialist must be aware of this most inconspicuous of all transformations.[11]

For Benjamin, the past is not to be rearticulated and presented "as it really was" but to be seized in a moment of danger, in that instant "when an image flashes up," when it can be recognized but never seen again. To retain an "image of the past which unexpectedly appears . . . singled out by history at a moment of danger" is to attempt to reckon with it, to see the past and to reveal the secret agreement between it and the present.[12] The scene of the public arrest of the Mexican gardener on the UC campus, the sentencing of twenty-five men in the Los Angeles courtroom, and the death of another within the structure of the prison system were moments of danger (for some of us) where the past of racial violence is recognizable in the present. In my field of vision, the cries of a mother in pain, the pleas of a father for his future, and the 185 years of life taken by the state are all images—memories that if positioned for reflection could reveal the continuity of racial violence that presently remains both seen and unseen.

The visual consumption or witnessing of punishment and discipline in the form of humiliation, trauma, and even death, as the *Red Record* indicates, has a history in this country. The disciplining of the racial body, and its spectacle as entertainment or evidence, has informed and formed race in the United States. From the photography of lynching that was used to shore up White power to the scalps and dismembered body parts of Native Americans acquired at the Battle of Stone Creek and put on display at the Apollo Theater in New York and saloons in Denver, Colorado, to the head of Joaquin Murrieta taken on tour to bars across California,[13] mutilated and degraded bodies of color have long been hoisted up the flag pole of White American supremacy to be gazed upon in the service of national becoming.

In the photo art book *Eyewitness at Wounded Knee*, a collection of over one hundred photos documenting the massacre, the authors provide a retelling of the history of the massacre by mapping the famous photos with lost firsthand testimonies and local agency reports.[14] To disrupt the state's story of Wounded Knee—one that indicted the Lakota people in their own massacre—the authors used the extensive interviews (of agency workers, teamsters, gravediggers, and Native peoples and settlers who lived through the event) collected by Eli Ricker, a judge and newspaper editor who refused to accept the official story. Heather Cox Richardson in the introduction explains that, in the aftermath of the massacre, the U.S. military demanded an investigation of James W. Forsyth, the leader of the Seventh Cavalry, who had disarmed the Lakota people, even though they had surrendered peacefully two days before, and in the massacre that followed lost 25 U.S. soldiers and 250 Lakota prisoners.[15] She states that then president Ben Harrison could not afford to take responsibility for the debacle or for prosecuting an army officer and that court officers were reluctant to prosecute one of their own, so Forsyth was exonerated on all counts. The photographs present the viewers, who become witnesses, with "people frozen in death, on a land frozen by cold, in pictures frozen in time."[16]

As forms of seeing and witnessing, *Without Sanctuary* and *COPS* are complex visual objects enlisted in the work of racial discipline. It is critical to understand the longer historical trajectory of spectacle and discipline to which they belong and what connects them to the complex way that the material value of White Humanity is created. To begin to see *COPS* and *Without Sanctuary* as both evidence and purveyor of the continued practice of racial discipline and violence and as part of a larger visual regime of spectacular violence, this chapter establishes a genealogy of *legal* and *extralegal* violence through a theoretical mirror held up to history.[17] Compelled by the moment of danger and Benjamin's call to seize memory, this chapter forces a reckoning of the past with its refracted present and examines the continued way in which we as a public "live with" the violent and destructive practice of racial discipline.

This forced reckoning begins by considering the conditions of possibility for racial discipline—the moments when material value is constituted through the disciplining of the racial body. This occurs within the terrain of crisis in which national becoming is answered in part by the criminalization of Black, Native American, Mexican, and Asian peoples and the visible disciplining of the racial body. This chapter, therefore, illuminates the reflected similarities between two historical periods—that of the era of Reconstruction and the simultaneous settling of the Southwest and that of the post-Fordist period of deindustrialization and globalization of late capital. Mapping the economic, political, and discursive terrain of each period and its material manifestation via the violently disciplined racial body makes clear the material value related to racial violence and the production of White Humanity. Each of these moments are a testament to the relations of the disciplined body to a national becoming.

The crowds that gathered to witness a lynching or attended the display of pieces of the racial body were, in a sense, standing vigil over the investment in their own material value. The turn of the twentieth and twenty-first centuries marked two violent periods in U.S. history when the disciplined and destroyed racial body played (as it continues to play today) a symbolic and material role in managing Crisis—the threat posed by the fully human, free, and liberated racial body to White Humanity. In this chapter, we first consider this historical mirror by extending Cheryl Harris's idea of Whiteness and its property value to explain the criminalization of raced and classed subjects that threatened material accumulation in the era of manifest destiny and the economic crisis that followed emancipation. Then, I lay out the material exigencies that motivated the shifting representations of the racial body in the South, West, and Southwest. Finally, I look at the consequences of those crises—the laws and policies articulated via the Black body during the Reconstruction era and in the post-1965 United States, and their effect, the devastation of the racial body.

The Red Record of Material Investment

The humiliation, degradation, and destruction of real human bodies in the name of punishment as seen in *Without Sanctuary* and *COPS*, in accordance with traditional American practices, is woven of the cloth that James Baldwin called simply America's history of racial terror.[18] This history of terror and brutality has often been masked as the meting out of justice and order and displayed for crowds as evidence of the stability of white supremacy.[19]

And, in the practice of bearing witness to brutalities in the name of law and order, a collective understanding of "sanctioned" violence emerged in the consolidation of a White public body. In the manner that Lauren Berlant attends to the "intimate domains of the quotidian" that form public identities, this consolidation had a material investment in the Black (or Other) body that was predicated not simply on its Blackness but on its punishment.[20]

The violence against the racial body in the name of justice that took place in public squares or city centers was generally the most extreme, often larger in terms of the size of crowds and the number of victims punished.[21] These publics, in a sense, were standing vigil over a materiality that was both bound to their racial identity and, in part, predicated on domination and economic accumulation organized by ideals of racial superiority.[22] Cheryl Harris tells us that the material value of Whiteness is founded in the history of U.S. nation building—a time period during which property rights became conflated with race and historical forms of domination over people of color had "evolved to reproduce the subordination of the present."[23] The material value inherent in a White racial identity, secured through a series of codes, laws, and policies that conflated race to legal definitions of property, conferred upon Whiteness the characteristics and material value of property.[24] The occupation or confiscation of land from American Indians, as well as the ownership of Black bodies, was legalized through a court system that provided legal protection of property, which would ultimately include protection by violent force.

By this account, Harris provides a way to consider the relationship between the transgression of the laws tied to property and personhood, such as the Slave Codes and Black Codes and various treaties, and the consequences of that transgression. In her mapping of Whiteness as material property, she states that it was through the legal regulation, the juridical administration of Blackness—of Black humanity—that the value of Whiteness is produced. The Slave Codes, the first laws regulating Blackness, ensured that Black people would be denied ownership and agency of their own personhood in order to maintain slavery's form of social relations and work to complete the commodification of human beings into alienable property. For Harris, "Slavery made human beings market alienable and in doing so, subjected human life and personhood—that which is most valuable—to the ultimate devaluation."[25] By market alienable, Harris means that Black personhood was turned into an external object of property. Therefore, to break the laws that bound personhood and identity to the economy and property was punishable by fines, lashes, or death.[26] The Slave Codes guaranteed Black alienation and servitude, and thus, the harshest penalties were reserved for acts that threatened the institution of slavery and the value bound to Whiteness. After emancipation, Southern and Northern states instituted Black Codes and Jim Crow laws that maintained those relations with equal if not more severe punishment for transgressions of the devaluation of the racial body.[27]

Although Harris illustrates the making of material value in a White personhood through law, she does not address the consequences of transgression—the criminalization of the free Black body and of the Native American body that dared defy reservation and treaty laws and the inherent violence in law required to maintain the protection of that value. Whiteness found value via the violent consequence: punishment of the body that transgressed the laws protecting White material value in property, personhood, and the expectation of that value. The bounty of that value was intimately bound up not simply with Blackness as its necessary opposite, for example, but with the suffering, degradation, humiliation, and destruction of that which could be attached to the body that dared transgress. The violent force of consequence and punishment (that is without measurement) ensures the protection of the value of Whiteness as property, which, citing Jeremy Bentham, is essentially "nothing but the basis of expectation."[28] As property is understood to be the child of law or the artifact of lawmaking, the inherent practice of the juridical protection of expectation (the ensured maintenance of value), it is the foundation of one's understanding of assured entitlement to protection in the future. Inherent in the idea of *expectation* in relation to law that being the projection of life beyond, there is an expected time of future where your future-self is assured and protected in law. As Harris states, citing Margaret Radin, "If an object you now control is bound up in your future plans or anticipation of your future self and it is partly these plans for your own continuity that make you a person then your personhood depends on the realization of these expectations."[29] To threaten this is to threaten the material value of the White future, the expectation of a fully protected life of potential, opportunity of hope, and posterity.

As a consequence, White material value was reaffirmed through the ritual extraction of humanity in body and in soul as a consequence. It is this process that, drawing on Wells, I call the Red Record of Material Value—the mutilated and destroyed human bodies that provide a record, both materially and symbolically, of the value of White accumulation in its own expectation of value as the embodiment of Humanity. This record can be read through the bodies of lynched Black people in the Reconstruction South, of lynched Mexican people in the Southwest, and through the broken and confined bodies of the 2.3 million incarcerated people in the contemporary United States.

At the turn of the twentieth century, this extraction of humanity had much of its efficacy in its visible and spectacular display. The disciplined and destroyed racial body, the actual material body, becomes a sign of state and white supremacist power and material accumulation in moments of fragility. This sign is intended to do both material and discursive work. The pieces of the body are presented as evidence and legitimation of the emerging state structures that would continue the practices of punishment as a means of ensuring stability. The acts of violence were not random: they were methodologically attached to the building of the structures designed to ensure the continued stability of existing political and economic relations.

Material Exigencies and Shifting Representations of the Racial Body

The end of the Civil War, which led to freed Black labor (after the passage of the Thirteenth Amendment), incited further crises in the Southern states. Scholars of the Reconstruction era explain that upon the freeing of Black slaves, the economic stability of Southern capital, already in a precarious state prior to and during the Civil War, was in ruin.[30] Although the response to this crisis was managed through a series of federal and state policies that would work to stabilize the South's economy, the most notable was the effort to reestablish the economic and social relationships instituted under slavery. The end of the Civil War left the South in a state of crisis.

The Southern states (although Arkansas is considered by some scholars an exception) were reeling from structural devastation in the form of the loss of basic capital—land and labor. Land value in almost every Southern state was in decline, which was seen in the mass auctioning of plantation property as well as the breaking down of plantations into growing units. Planters became landlords, dividing the cultivation of their land among cash tenants and fragmenting the plantation, which was predicated on a world of scarce capital and abundant labor.[31] The marketing of cotton was decentralized. Farmers now sold products to traders and peddlers versus larger commission merchants. Southern states such as Tennessee borrowed substantial sums of money to finance improvements, especially the development of railroads. Radical unionists increased debt to the point that it became a major political issue between the Southern state governments.

Making due note of the precarious period in which freed Black persons were dangerously suspended in an emancipated/nonemancipated state, Du Bois points out that upon the ratification of the Thirteenth Amendment, the question regarding the civil and human status of Black people was answered by the Black Codes, a set of laws that were, in his words, an "indisputable attempt to make Negroes slaves in everything but name."[32] These codes, their enforcement, and the legal and extralegal public practice of lynching were visible markers of work to reestablish the economic and social order in the South.

This work of emancipation/nonemancipation took place on the terrain of both representation and law. In the antebellum South, the prevailing discourse regarding the status and condition of Black slaves and their humanity is best surmised in a paper delivered by Dr. Thomas Henry Huxley to the Ladies' London Emancipation Society, in which he declared that the body of the "Negro that is before you is clearly incapable of erect posture."[33] This representation of the so-called subhuman features of Black people as "more akin to animals" prevailed, along with the images of pastoral scenes of slave life on the plantation. According to Everette James, pictorial depictions of African Americans by White people in the South evoked these pastoral scenes to represent the Black minstrel as an unthreatening figure—the lazy, childlike, imbecilic slave or the happy-go-lucky Sambo, humorous and nonthreatening.[34] These representations of Black people articulated a humanity that was not to be taken seriously. These representations of Black people as property in law and culture became part of the visual landscape of the postwar era.

After the Civil War, the Reconstruction Crisis brought with it a shift in ideology. In addressing the status of free Black people in the Southern as well as the Northern states, President Andrew Johnson, who vetoed both the Freedman's Bureau and the first civil rights bill drawn up by Senator Lyman Trumbull to address the Black Codes of the states, famously proclaimed, "This is a country for white men, and by God, as long as I am President, it shall be a government for white men." It served as an answer to the purgatorial status of Black citizenship and equality. The struggle to discursively represent the newly freed Black population was intended to deny Black people their freedom. This sentiment was shared in the North, where the Pennsylvania governor stated that "this is still a white man's government . . . and the Negro must be made to understand that freedom does not mean idleness and vagrancy."[35]

It is no coincidence that during this time period, a dangerous shift in the representation of Black people emerged. The development of the threatening prototype of the Black male prevailed and would most notoriously appear as Gus in D. W. Griffith's 1915 movie *Birth of a Nation*. After emancipation and the end of the abolitionist or proslavery arguments, the docile or happy-go-lucky imaginary of Black people was no longer necessary. The image of the Black rapist or black-as-beast prevailed into the twentieth century.[36] According to Sandra Gunning:

Cultural producers (those for and against white supremacy) were compelled to re-invent the South after Reconstruction by re-envisioning race relations for a new era. . . . They engage fully with the figures of the black rapist in order to delineate post–civil war identities of black and white. . . . This became a forum for the virtual obsession with the black male body.[37]

This representation proved to be dangerous, as it also mixed easily with discourses of biology and difference and virulent anti-miscegenation laws enacted during the same period.

A parallel shift occurred in the representations of Mexicans, Native Americans, and Chinese during the same period. The history of material accumulation and investment in Whiteness necessitated the creation of raced representations of these groups and their simultaneous physical destruction. During the time period prior to the Civil War and the decades following it, the doctrine of manifest destiny flourished. At its center was the idea of Anglo-Saxon innate superiority. The acquisition of Texas, New Mexico, Arizona, and California furthered the projects of transportation and export and the development of new industries. California was important to maritime traders due to the earliest West Coast ports and access to the Pacific Rim. In 1830, an overland route was established from Santa Fe, New Mexico, to California. In the east and central valleys of Texas, cattle grazing began as a staple economic activity, and, by 1820, the extension of cotton culture made its way into central and south Texas. As cotton became increasingly important to Southern capital, the increase in the Anglo population prompted the Mexican government to pass the Colonization Law, which prohibited slavery in Texas and curtailed the rapidly growing number of Anglos moving into Texas. Anglos resented the imposition of the Mexican government on trade into Louisiana and the East Coast, and some scholars contend that Southern growers instigated the annexation of Texas to incorporate a new slave state into the union.[38]

Although the sentiments of manifest destiny began in the early 1830s, it flourished during the Mexican-American War and prevailed by the 1850s, justifying the violent domination, land dispossession, political disenfranchisement, and labor exploitation of the inhabitants of the Southwest.[39] As Anglo-Saxons were regarded as a separate and superior race destined to bring good government and commercial prosperity to the continent of America, the idea of Mexicanness as a racial category emerged.[40] Mexicans were regarded as barbarous half-breeds. Having inherited the worst traits of the Spanish and Indians (i.e., as Mestizos), they were mongrels and thus inferior. Mexicans were considered more Indian than European, and their European blood was of an inferior brand, as they presumably carried the Black blood of the Moors through their Spanish lineage. They were seen as a superstitious and backward people, incapable of utilizing the land and, therefore, in need of governance. David J. Weber documents the perceptions of Mexicans when Anglos first encountered them in the 1820s. The idea that Mexicans were "scarce more than apes" prevailed in the Southwest. According to Weber, Stephen Austin called the people that he encountered in the Texas territory "bigoted and superstitious to an extreme. . . . The whole nation as far as I have seen them want nothing more than tails to be more brutes than apes."[41]

Nowhere was this more apparent than in Texas, where the earliest policing of Mexicans by the Texas Rangers was a brutal and violent practice considered necessary to the settlement of the state. Border Mexicans were commonly perceived as cruel and treacherous, as cowardly thieves by nature due to their mixed-race ancestry, and as an eminent danger to the White settlers of the Southwest.[42] They were portrayed in newspapers and by historians as cowardly and backstabbing thieves and bandits, whereas the Rangers were portrayed as heroic and brave defenders of White Texans who could take on a whole Mexican town with one bullet.[43]

Americo Paredes tells us that the historical function of representations that villainize groups has been to condone the violence of ideological economic projects that necessitate the domination of the racial subject. He states of myth and representation: "One notes that the White southerner took his slave women as concubines and then created an image of the male Negro as a sex fiend. In the same way he appears to have taken the Mexican's property and made him out a thief."[44] For the cattle barons of nineteenth-century Texas and their protectors, the Texas Rangers, it was the Border Mexican who became the symbolic representation of that which stood in the way of the complete and total acquisition of Texas.

The lynching of Mexican people in the Southwest and in California, although not documented to the same extent as the lynching targeting Black people, was extensive. Between 1848 and 1879, an estimated 473 per 100,000 Mexican people were lynched at the hands of mobs in Texas, New Mexico, Arizona, California, and Colorado.[45]

Alongside the parallel shift that was occurring in the representations of Mexican and Black people, Native Americans were represented in increasingly criminalized frames. The conquest of lands and the resulting oppression and violence perpetrated against Native Americans was validated by the discourse and policy of westward expansion. Earlier representations of the Native American as the noble savage, influence the cult of Primitivism in which the Native American appears uncorrupted by civilization, unthreatening, and enlightened by their proximity to nature,[46] were replaced by the image of the bad Indian, a marauding and untamable murderer who scalped women and children. Once destroyed or relegated to the reservation, Native peoples were depicted as thieves, drunks, and beggars. Luanna Ross explains that, as the material stakes in Montana were high, the acquisition of land for copper was a violent process that depended on the "creation of bad Indians."[47] Montana alone held 21 percent of the world's copper as well as valuable land for cattle grazing. While the population of White people in Montana exploded from 39,000 to 143,000, the Native population was drastically reduced through disease and displacement. While Native Americans were driven into abject poverty, by 1894, Helena had more millionaires per capita than any other city in the United States.[48]

The national sentiment toward Native Americans was exemplified in President Roosevelt's expression of his solution to the "Indian Problem." Roosevelt stated, "I suppose I should be ashamed to say that I take the Western view of the Indian. I don't go so far as to think that the only good Indians are dead Indians, but I believe nine out of every ten are. . . . [They are] reckless, revengeful, fiendishly cruel, they rob and murder."[49] Roosevelt's nationalism expressed itself as a combative and unapologetic racial ideology that thrived on aggression and the vanquishing of "savage" and "barbaric peoples." The extermination of the Native American relied on the criminalization of their racial entity.[50]

As forms of racial discipline emerged through this visuality of violence, the Black, Mexican, and Native American people were rendered as dangerous threats alongside the Chinese immigrants. Chinese immigrants faced discrimination in many areas of law, including state and local tax laws, city business ordinances, work licensing requirements, and criminal laws and policies. The fear of Chinese labor competition was amplified by the prevailing notion that the Chinese were racially inferior, inherently unassimilable, and dangerous to the communities in which they lived.[51] The Chinese were rendered as a dangerous threat to labor in the West and suffered the violence of mobs from the northwestern states to the South. In California, the Order of the Caucasians, the Working Man's Party, and the Democratic Party rounded up and expelled or killed Chinese immigrants and Chinese Americans. This violence was accompanied by the sensationalistic discourse of the "Yellow Peril," as newspapers and early novels depicted the Chinese as devious creatures whose control over certain businesses and willingness to work for low wages put White workers out of work.

The early criminalization of opium also demonized the Chinese in racial terms, so that savagery and danger were perceived as inherent. According to Jimmie Reeves and Richard Campbell, "Savage competition between these factions of the labor market helped inspire mean spirited ordinances that were meant to punish the Chinese for, well, being Chinese."[52] Reeves and Campbell claim that the opium issue was part of an ideological response to a labor market crisis and, further, assert that the practical consequence of the antiopium campaign was to provide a legal basis for unrestrained and arbitrary police raids and searches of Chinese premises in San Francisco.[53] The legal targeting of Black, Mexican, Native American, and Chinese people occurred alongside textual and visual representations of these groups as dangerous and threatening to White Humanity.

The Mirror at Work

This is the geohistorical and political economic terrain—one of slavery, dispossession, genocide, and war—on which we witness the twenty-first-century practices of racial state violence in COPS and *Without Sanctuary*, and it is the mirror up to which we can hold the present accountable for the work of criminalization. These forms of the criminalization of the racial body, motivated by material crises and opportunities, remained particularly and cruelly evident in the era of late capital and neoliberalism. This era was marked by the early stages of the U.S. economic restructuring, including deindustrialization and deregulation, which resulted in permanent elevated levels of unemployment and the loss of community infrastructure that severely affected individuals already disenfranchised from the mainstream workforce.[54] Referred to by Barry Bluestone and Bennett Harrison as the "widespread systematic disinvestments in the nation's basic productive capacity," the crisis of the 1970s and 1980s can be traced to the move of capital from productive investment in basic national industries into unproductive speculation, mergers and acquisitions, and foreign investment.[55] This disinvestment shifted the economic terrain in a manner that would undergird the new era of social and political relations.[56] The economic changes in the United States since the late 1970s have been a major source of economic insecurity, including new forms of employment-centered poverty, especially, although not exclusively, in urban centers where "the majority (of the population) [was] linked to decaying domestic institutions while a small, privileged elite pursued its accumulation drives within global networks."[57] This also led to the polarization of service industries and the casualization of employment, resulting in the creation of a remarginalized urban population.[58] These polarizations were accompanied by discursive images of villainous Japanese workers and car companies blamed for the loss of U.S. auto industry jobs.[59]

At the same time, government officials, neoconservative think tanks, and academics found ways to justify the economic crisis of the 1970s. George Gilder, author of *Wealth and Poverty*, and other secular theologians warned of an insidious moral decadence overtaking the country.[60] The crisis of U.S. capital was simply a matter of a lack of commitment, innovation, and "old fashioned" hard work, which required a correction of morals and ethics.[61] The crisis of morality, or what was referred to as the loss of "the psychological means of production," held a place in the public mind. Conservatives faulted individuals for their lack of moral self-discipline as the cause of the economic crisis.

In this economic context, the prevailing political rationale was the neoconservative view of big government. David Stockman, director of Reagan's

Office of Management and Budget, claimed that high taxes, openhanded welfare programs, and business regulations were barriers to economic recovery.[62] Conservatives alleged that big government discouraged hard work, saving money, and new productive investment, and their agenda resulted in the dismantling of the state welfare support system in the midst of a new economic era. Relying on the discursive image of the welfare queen and her offspring, Reagan dismantled the social welfare state while increasing spending on the security apparatus at all levels of government. This warfare apparatus targeted the inner-city violence and pathology that became a discursive emblem of the Reagan-Bush era.

As the Cold War came to an end with the televisual imagery of newly united Germans tearing down the Berlin Wall in 1989, the United States declared war against a new enemy. Changes in international politics opened an ideological space for a form of racialized fear that would materialize in the mass incarceration of Black, Brown, and poor White people at unprecedented levels. The external enemy, against which the United States identified and imagined itself, was transformed into an internal racial enemy in the ideological formations of immigration, drugs, crime, and welfare.[63] The Red Record of Material Value would continue across the centuries, both in the racial imagery of the 1980s and 1990s and in the massive levels of incarceration that we as a public watched on our televisions in the form of programming and news.

Another critical moment in the production of the visual narrative of race and crime was Republican candidate George H. W. Bush's election campaign of 1988, which, as part of a political "show," rendered an image of crime in full color. Supplying the public with a highly visible enemy, Bush's campaign used an ad produced by the National Security Action Committee that featured photographs of Bush and his opponent, Michael Dukakis, framed as contestants in the fight against crime. Dukakis was presented as soft on crime in ads that flashed a photograph of a Black male on the screen, as an announcer stated, "Dukakis not only opposes the death penalty, he allowed first-degree murderers to have weekend passes from prison. One was Willie Horton, who murdered a boy in a robbery, stabbing him nineteen times. Despite a life sentence, Horton received ten weekend passes from prison. Horton fled, kidnapped a young couple, stabbing the man and repeatedly raping his girlfriend."[64] This ad ran for twenty-eight days on cable television across the nation. The ad, without an explicit racial discourse, clearly illustrated the color of crime as Black through the photograph of Horton, and the Whiteness of the victims. In the political televisual world, the War on Crime positioned Horton as its Black signifier at a turning point in a televised political anticrime agenda that had actually developed over the previous decades. In the minds of Americans, Horton's face took its place alongside images of inner-city welfare mothers, gangbangers, violent robbers, and urban carjackers—the "them" opposing "us" in the war against any threat to White Humanity.

The Reagan-Bush era left a legacy of hypervisual divisions and demarcations: American versus foreigner/infiltrator/invader, Black versus White, and rich versus poor. As explained by Michael Rogin, Reagan represented to the public "the benign center of America" and "placed malignancies outside our borders."[65] These borders were set up internally as well, dividing who and what represented America from all that was evil and anti-American. During this time, the trilogy of films that told the story of John Rambo, Vietnam veteran turned fighter of foreign terrorists, was a powerful box office draw, and the success of *Top Gun* created a new, also militarized, American action hero. In addition to the big-screen presentation of American patriotism, U.S. audiences also consumed the soap opera–like unfoldment of the O. J. Simpson trial, the Rodney King beating, and the 1992 Los Angeles rebellion.

The viewing of crime and punishment by national audiences was, of course, accompanied by continuously changing laws and policies tailored for inner-city populations. Federal and state programs funded full-scale police sweeps focused on the neighborhoods perceived to be overrun with gangs.[66] Local, state, and federal policies that targeted the "gang problem" also contained and incarcerated Black and Latino (and increasingly Asian) youths who were perceived as gang initiated or gang affiliated. Policing structures were poised and ready to contain the new "enemy within" as sensationalized incidents of violence in cities like Los Angeles appeared on the nightly news. These dramatic changes in crime policy and the dramatization and visualization of crime can be understood by the production of the "internal enemy," the Bloods and Crips gang members, inner-city carjackers, and crack cocaine dealers and users who came to signify the racial body.[67]

Visual narratives in the War on Drugs took on hyperbolic levels of panic and indignation as crack cocaine took center stage. The war was always visual: when Nancy Reagan joined an LAPD Special Forces Unit in a drug raid of a home in South Central Los Angeles, it was televised and broadcast all over the country. She appeared alongside Daryl Gates, wearing blue jeans and an LAPD police jacket bearing the words "The Establishment," at a raid accompanied by tanks and helicopters.[68] In 1986, upon the unexpected deaths of nationally known athletes Len Bias and Don Rogers, who both died from cocaine overdoses, the Massachusetts Democratic congressman Tip O'Neill launched a massive campaign against drug use. By using the deaths of the clean-cut young Black all-American athletes as "color-blind" reasoning to begin the largest discursive crime war in the United States, the antidrug campaign was a matter of racial discipline turned into spectacle.[69]

The Record Itself: Consequences of the Racial Body

The visual and discursive representations of the racial body as threatening enabled a set of laws and policies that integrated race as an inherent component. In the Reconstruction era, the Black Codes set a precedent for laws in which the visibility of the body played a central role. In the purportedly color-blind post–civil rights era, this task became more complicated, as laws and policies translated the visibility of the racial body through the discourse of drugs and the fear of violence. The result was a contemporary analogue to the Black Codes or the pass system and other mobility-regulating laws and policies. In both periods, the nation endured a perceived crisis. Laws and policies were instituted to manage that crisis via the bodies of the poor and people of color.

During the crisis of Reconstruction, the early laws that criminalized the newly free Black people were marked by the intensely violent practices of white supremacy, which required the visible evidence of its work. Spanning almost fifty years, the Slave Codes came to an end in 1865, as Black people were freed and given the right to marry and enter into contracts.[70] The Black Codes were a rearticulation of the way the Slave Codes controlled and criminalized the behavior of the newly freed Black population. The freeing of enslaved Black labor disrupted the stability and order of the South's economy and social relations, and the immediate response was, according to Angela Davis, to quickly "develop a criminal justice system that could legally restrict the possibilities of freedom for newly released slaves."[71]

Prior to the Civil War, the consequences of crimes committed by slaves were the responsibility of their owners and largely occurred outside of the legal system. With the Black Codes, freed Black people were policed, arrested, and imprisoned within the confines of the American penal system. As state-level laws throughout the South, these codes varied only slightly from the Slave Codes. Their guiding principle was to restrict the movement of Black bodies and labor. The effects of the Black Codes were particularly *seen* manifestations; they, in large part, depended on the visibility of the body. They were enacted in the public arena—city streets, country roads, agricultural fields, and churches—as a theater in which Blackness as a visible marker became a dangerous liability.

The Black Codes, which varied from state to state, provided the legal foundation for newly freed Black people to remain in a nonemancipated state. Both Mississippi and South Carolina had large Black populations and the most severe Black Codes. In these states, as well as in the rest of the South, the Black Codes reflected white planter anxiety over freed Black men. Du Bois describes the codes as an "indisputable attempt to make Negroes slaves in everything but name."[72] These laws, which regulated interstate migration, employment, and city curfew and prohibited the consumption of alcohol, carrying weapons, vagrancy, gambling, and congregating with others, all carried a punishment of either a fine, hard labor, or imprisonment.[73] They also outlawed mobility and deputized White citizens as police. A partial list of the Louisiana Black Codes reads:

> Section 1. Be it ordained by the police jury of St. Landry, that no negro shall be allowed to pass within the limits of the said parish without special permit in writing. . . .
>
> Section 6. No negro who is not in the military service shall be allowed to carry firearms or any kind of weapons. . . .
>
> Section 11. It shall be the duty of every citizen to act as a police officer for the detection of offenses and the apprehension of offenders.[74]

The regulation of mobility and the codification of White public policing were key features of the codes. Crossing boundaries, such as city limits or even designated neighborhoods, was a criminal act, punishable by a fine that was to be paid by hard labor. In state courts, the regulation of Black movement was explained as a response to the fear of increased Black criminal activity, as was the outlawing of firearms for Black people and the need for every white citizen to police these codes. Every basic right granted to white citizens was conversely denied to Black people. In essence, it was illegal for Black people to work, marry, congregate, or protect their persons or property—any reproductive human practice was a criminal act. And it was the job of the White public to mete out the disciplinary consequences in front of the eyes of White viewers. As Du Bois explains, the earliest policing of Black people in the South was performed by poor white people: "The system of slavery demanded a special police force and such a force was made possible and unusually effective by the presence of the poor whites. . . . The planters formed proportionately quite a small class but they had singularly enough at their command some five million poor whites."[75]

The public arena in which the Black body was under constant surveillance ensured the importance of visualizing the racial body in a particular way. The body engaged in the motions of freedom—walking the streets, purchasing goods, attending church—provided the evidence that would establish its criminality and, hence, its necessary punishment. The codes that criminalized Blackness were an attempt to manage the crisis of the free Black body, and, in doing so, established a way of seeing it, in all its freedom, as a transgression and a threat to the value of Whiteness.

The codes legitimated the regulation of the free/emancipated body by law and by force. Within the contradictions of freedom versus the reality of a rearticulated slavery, the body appeared as evidence of stability. Because these codes were established in the first moments of the freeing of the Black body, they outlawed the very being of that racial body. As a consequence, the criminalization, policing, and imprisonment of Black people assured a response to the turbulent social and economic crisis of the Reconstruction era. At the same time as the Thirteenth Amendment called for the end of slavery, it also declared that punishment for a criminal act would result in a continuation of the body being owned and valued for its labor. The first section states: "Neither slavery nor involuntary servitude, except as a punishment for crime whereof the party shall have been duly convicted, shall exist within the United States, or any place subject to their jurisdiction." This exception, to commit a convict to involuntary servitude as criminal punishment, was an attempt to replicate the power dynamics of unpaid labor, if not in actual imprisonment then certainly ideologically.[76]

These codes resulted in a striking shift in the makeup of imprisoned populations. According to Mary Ellen Curtin, prior to the Civil War, penitentiaries in the South were overwhelmingly populated by white males; they were, in fact, almost 96 percent white.[77] Within five years after the Civil War ended, the population of Southern penal institutions became almost completely Black, transforming the ideal of free Black labor into the structure of convict leasing and the chain gang, a form of labor that was, according to scholars, more exploitative, inhumane, and terrifying than slavery itself.[78]

The early chain gang and convict leasing system produced a new type of labor regime that both facilitated the rebuilding of the South and relied on and necessitated the criminalization of Black people. Alabama's state prison system, for example, was 99 percent white before the Civil War but overwhelmingly Black twenty years later. The notorious Mississippi "Pig Law" of 1876 made the stealing of a pig a criminal act of grand larceny subject to five years in the state penitentiary and resulted in the increase of Black state convicts from 272 in 1874 to 1,072 in 1877. Lichtenstein suggests that the convict leasing system in conjunction with the Black Codes and Jim Crow laws was such a significant development that it contributed to the advancement of a racial state.[79]

Mancini describes the convict leasing system from its inception after the Civil War to its ending in the early twentieth century as resembling the darkest days of colonial indentured servitude. It was the principal means by which Southern states could meet the private labor needs of sugar, cotton, and tobacco plantations, coal and phosphate mines, turpentine farms, and sawmills.[80] And, although Mancini's analysis centers the cost of labor as the driving force of convict labor, he explains that race ruled the fate of the convicts. The harshest convict leasing practices existed in Alabama, Georgia, Louisiana, and Mississippi, where the system found support among white people who saw a return to the natural social order in the "long rows of stooped Black bodies working in gangs."[81] These gangs toiled under the watchful eye and quick whip of the state overseer whose work it was to ensure economic profit. David Oshinsky explains that the convict leasing system in Mississippi amounted to nothing less than state-run slavery as it paid convicts $1.10 per month and would sublease each convict for $9.00 per month to plantation owners across the state.[82]

As the Southern penal system increasingly resembled the practices of slave bondage, and Black people became Black prisoners in vast numbers, whippings were instituted as prison practices of control and punishment.[83] The whip, the overseer, and "drivers" who worked the convicts in the fields of Mississippi followed the direction of state governor James E. Vardaman, who "stood out among racist demagogues of the era—or any era—for his inflammatory rhetoric, his open support of lynching and his promises to protect white people from the 'brutish biological failings' of the 'colored race.'"[84] Laboring prisoners were punished, according to Oshinsky, "for; 'slow hoeing' (ten lashes), 'sorry planting' (five lashes), and 'being light with cotton' (five lashes)." The continuity of drivers with whips and overseers on horseback was part of the visual display of racial discipline that symbolically represented the natural social order of White control and supremacy of the South.

The Mirror Facing History

As an analogous process occurring a century later, with equally disastrous and painful consequences, the punitive policies of the post-1965 era were not unlike the Black Codes. Although each of the fifty states continues to determine its own crime laws, the federal "get tough on crime" stance of the late 1960s trickled down to local levels with the passing of seven federal crime bills. These federal bills were used to influence state crime policies by withholding monies from state and local governments unless they adopted certain "get tough" measures. Between the earliest and costliest crime bill—the Safe Streets Act, which concentrated on social discord and "chaos"—and the Clinton-era crime bills of the 1990s, federal crime policies shifted their focus to the perceived drug crisis instead of the fear of social upheaval. These crime bills were a direct response to the panic and fear of drugs and crime-related violence, and they changed the practice of policing, the racial composition of the criminal justice system, and the political landscape of incarceration in the United States.

Although, in the popular imagination, the wars against drugs and crime are seen as emblematic of the Reagan reign, the increase in spending to accommodate them rested on a foundation of state restructuring that began a decade and a half earlier, at the same time that massive economic restructuring began to take shape in the 1970s. In the 1980s, funding for the justice system at the federal, state, and local levels exploded, with the average direct local, state, and federal expenditures for police increasing by 416 percent. The growth of more modern policing structures, organizations, and institutions and the new discourse on crime known as Nancy's War stems from the large-scale state and policing structures built to control and contain populations that were resistant to their immediate social and economic conditions.[85]

Before the Reagan reign, a new era of anti-crime rhetoric had already emerged. During the 1964 Republican presidential primary campaign between George Wallace and Barry Goldwater, the segregationist Wallace espoused a tough-on-crime platform, which had not been heard as a leading discourse since the Prohibition era. Goldwater adopted this rhetoric and declared that there was a threat of lawlessness running through the nation, which, in turn, forced Lyndon B. Johnson to address lawlessness in his presidential reelection campaign.[86] Johnson promised to create a commission, called the Commission on Law Enforcement and Administration of Justice, which was to study and make recommendations for solving the rising crime problem in the United States. Shortly thereafter, the Watts rebellion broke out, marking the beginning of a series of urban uprisings that represented a growing sentiment of dissent and resistance to state power.[87] As the United States was in the midst of a social revolution, the government responded by linking dissent to criminality.

The present anti-crime police state and structures of mass incarceration grew out of that link. According to Christian Parenti, Congress worked hard in the wake of the Martin Luther King Jr. and Robert Kennedy assassinations and the Watts riots to help craft and pass Johnson's Omnibus Crime Control and Safe Streets Act. This act landed Johnson $75 million in overall crime-prevention spending (with a majority of the money to be used for riot control and police training) and "draconian legal provisions," which weakened the basic features of Miranda rights in federal cases and cleared the way for similar laws at the state level.[88] The Safe Streets Act initiated the professionalization and militarization of local police forces by applying military and weapons technology developed for Vietnam to urban policing settings across the country. Additionally, the act initiated modern management techniques to reorganize police forces into more professionalized units assisted by a new federal agency (also funded under the Safe Streets Act), the Law Enforcement Assistance Administration (LEAA). The LEAA was initially set up as an advisory organization to counsel and assist local police departments across the country. Ultimately, it was the LEAA that provided departments with helicopters and other forms of military technology to deal with what was seen as an impending urban crisis.[89]

As the social fabric of the country was thought to be coming apart at the seams, President Richard Nixon attempted to make good on his law and order platform with anti-crime legislation to fight a drug problem plaguing all of the United States and even contributing to its problems in the Vietnam War.[90] In 1970, Congress passed the Comprehensive Drug Abuse Prevention and Control Act and allotted the Bureau of Narcotics and Dangerous Drugs three hundred additional agents. That same year, Congress allotted the LEAA $3.5 billion to be distributed to local and state law enforcement over the next three years. As Nixon's War on Drugs campaign began, he signed the Organized Crime Control Bill (better known as the Racketeer Influenced and Corrupt Organizations Act), which was initiated to dismantle several East Coast organized crime families but was soon used against leftist activists. The Department of Justice under Nixon subpoenaed thousands of individuals identified as resistant to Nixon's agenda. Parenti explains that journalists and members of the Black Panthers and the Puerto Rican *Independistas* were brought before grand juries resulting from the Racketeer Influenced and Corrupt Organizations Act, illustrating the fact that Nixon's real enemies were the urbanized poor. Parenti cites the diary of Nixon's chief of staff H. R. Haldeman: "[President Nixon] emphasized that you have to face the fact that the whole problem is really the blacks. The key is to devise a system that recognizes this while not appearing to."

During the early 1970s, the LEAA was the fastest-growing agency in the federal government. Fifty percent of the agency's action grants were allotted to purchase local police hardware and police training in an attempt to deal with crime, the protest movement, and inner-city rioting. The demands of local police departments were met with increased congressional funding for the LEAA because of growing concerns over the ability of police to deal with urban resistance. To receive funds, each state was required to form a planning agency with the intent to modernize and professionalize its policing structures and to have the local police planning body approved by the LEAA. The LAPD (in response to Watts) was one of the first to receive funding and embrace the more modern managerial models and wartime hardware to correct its perceived failures in policing social resistance, which had by then come to be called crime.[91] As in the post-Reconstruction era, social crises were resolved through the criminalization of the racial body, and we could soon watch it on *COPS*.

As Nixon's administration ended, it left behind the economic and political foundation of what became known as the Reagan administration's War on Drugs. Notably, the Office of Drug Abuse Law Enforcement, a new policing agency that, for the first time in history, answered directly to the White House, was later merged with the Bureau of Narcotics and Dangerous Drugs to create the federal Drug Enforcement Agency and was allotted another

$3.5 billion to last until the mid-1970s with a significant portion of these monies (approximately $268 million) going to the LEAA. When Reagan signed the 1984 Comprehensive Crime Control Act, it overhauled federal sentencing procedures and revised bail and forfeiture policies. Its major impact on policing and incarceration was the allocation of federal monies to the local police for drug and crime prevention. Reagan followed this crime bill with a federal antidrug bill that would illustrate the most marked racial formation of the criminal justice system in the twentieth century.

In 1988, Congress overwhelmingly passed the Drug Abuse Act, which was signed by the president in mid-October. The bill allotted $124.5 billion, a significant portion of which was earmarked for new prison construction. Sixty million dollars was to go to the Drug Enforcement Agency and $230 million for state and local law enforcement, which translated into a massive increase in narcotics arrests. The bill imposed twenty-nine new mandatory minimum sentences against certain drug offenses and denied probation or suspended sentences to individuals convicted of new crimes. The most remarkable provision in the act was the discrepancy in sentencing for the use and sale of different forms of cocaine. For offenses involving 100 grams of heroin or 500 grams of cocaine, there was a minimum sentence of five years. For one hundredth of that amount, or five grams of crack cocaine, the sentence was the same. In a criminal legal system that cost over $200 billion annually by the 1990s, this translated into what Parenti calls apartheid sentencing, as Black people were more frequently arrested and charged with the use and sale of crack cocaine rather than powder cocaine.[92]

In 1994, when President Clinton passed the Violent Crime Control and Law Enforcement Act, it allocated $23 billion for law enforcement and included a provision that increased the number of crimes punishable by death. The most significant provision of the act was policing grants totaling $8.8 billion for the hiring of one hundred thousand new officers, purchasing of equipment, and establishing of community policing programs to complement the newly designed drug laws. For state prison building, $7.9 billion in federal matching funds were allotted. The crime bill also established a federal sentencing commission directed to increase penalties and institute mandatory sentencing guidelines for the manufacturing and selling of drugs in newly designated "drug free zones." Under this act, federal capital punishment was expanded to sixteen new crimes and a "three strikes" provision was enacted. New federal sentencing enhancements for individuals categorized as gang members were instituted, and, for the first time, the federal government was authorized to aid states in instituting laws to enable courts to try juveniles as adults. In addition, the Border Patrol received $1.2 billion to hire four thousand new agents.

Much like the shift in prison populations that occurred in the postbellum South, the drastic increase in the prison population was mobilized around a racial discourse that had profound and horrifying consequences for people of color and the poor. At the same time that economic restructuring and globalization were adversely affecting people of color, women, and the poor in the United States, the prison population increased to historically unprecedented levels. According to the U.S. Department of Justice, the total U.S. prison population in 1968 was 187,000. In just over ten years, the number had risen to 329,821 persons in both state and federal prisons. However, it was during the 1980s and 1990s that the most dramatic increase occurred. In 1982, when the national crime rate was the lowest it had been in over twenty years, the total prison population was 405,962. By 1994, the prison population had nearly tripled to 1,182,169, and by the year 2000 that number had increased to 2,071,686 people. Prison growth remained steady over the next few years, with a slight rise in 2003 and 2004. Between mid-2003 and mid-2004, 900 inmates were imprisoned each week, and, by 2006, the U.S. prison population hovered at almost 2.3 million people.[93]

The racial configuration of imprisonment remains burdened by the legacies of past relations between the state, economic interests, policing, and punishment (and the way in which we live with acute racial discrimination that has been naturalized over time). While Black people make up only 12 percent of the general population, of the over 2 million prisoners in the United States, 47 percent are Black. While white people accounted for 70 percent of the population, they make up only 35 percent of the total prison population. For every 100,000 people in the United States, 2,531 Black people are imprisoned compared to 393 white people. This disparity is even more severe if we account for gender. And for every 100,000 people, 4,919 Black males are incarcerated compared to 717 white males. The picture is even more dire when age is factored in—for Black males ages 25–29, 12,603 per 100,000 are behind bars (which is 12 percent of the Black male population) as opposed to 1,666 white males of the same age group.[94] A study conducted by the National Center for Institutions and Alternatives found that, in 1992, 42 percent of all Black males between 18 and 35 years of age, in Washington, DC, were incarcerated. In that same year, nearly one-third of all Black males in Los Angeles County had already been jailed at least once. According to Human Rights Watch, Black men are incarcerated at more than ten times the rate of white males in thirteen states. In California, for every 139 white male prison admissions, there are 669 Black admissions; in Illinois, for every 20 white prison admissions, there are 1,146 Black admissions; in Maryland, for every 22 white admissions there are 628 Black admissions; and, in Ohio, for every 34 white people, 968 Black people are incarcerated.

These figures—and the overwhelmingly repressive reality they represent—signify, if anything does, a moment of danger in Benjamin's sense. Through them, we can recognize the painful continuity of racial discipline in U.S. history and all of its attendant suffering and loss of life. Though this continuity would go unseen by most of its viewers, the mirror held to history could be seen in a remarkable photography exhibit in March 2000 on the walls of a Manhattan gallery.

PART II

3

WITHOUT SANCTUARY

A Moment of Opportunity

I don't know why we are even carrying it. . . . What do we
need this for? I can't believe it even happened here. I
couldn't even touch it. I had George set up the display.

—A YOUNG WOMAN IN HER TWENTIES TO
HER OLDER COWORKER

Well I know that it's horrible . . . but people can learn from
it, I guess. I mean we have come a long way and we should
appreciate living in a country where we've come so far from
such terrible things.

—AN OLDER COWORKER IN RESPONSE TO
THE YOUNG WOMAN

In the spring of 2000, I was in a La Jolla, California, bookstore and heard
two employees having the just-cited conversation about a recent arrival
in a newly received shipment. Both women, clearly disturbed and anx-
ious, continued consoling each other as I walked over to the display table they
referred to and saw for the first time the book *Without Sanctuary: Lynching
Photography in America*. I was shocked, too, by its intimidating and grim
cover: highly stylized, all black, with a long rectangular photo of a young man
hanging from a tree as several faces below him—two men and a boy—looked
up smiling. I was overwhelmed by what I saw. Upon opening the cover, I became witness to violence beyond explanation even for me.

At the turn of the twenty-first century, *Without Sanctuary* rightly drew
attention across the country as both a book and a museum exhibition. Reviews and reactions ranged from shock, disbelief, and guilt to anger and dis-
illusion. However, the resounding sentiment, once the shock dissipated, was
the same sense of acknowledged triumph over the violent brutality of an un-
civilized society. As noted, I heard one of the bookstore workers express, with
a sense of uncomfortable relief, "But we can learn from it. We've come so far
from such terrible things." These acts and practices had apparently been relegated to some dark past of U.S. history, one that was irrational, frenzied, and
backward, a history that had passed, one that "we" as a country had over-

come. And it was a history, according to one newspaper reviewer, that *needed to be seen* in order to not be repeated as well as to acknowledge "how complex and ingrained in the human psyche the capacity to go horrendously haywire is."[1]

The experience in the bookstore was telling. I too felt that the "reality" captured in the horrifying photos hardly seemed real. I shared with others an inability to comprehend this level of violence—images of men hanging one after the other, bodies stripped and beaten, and dismembered and burned bodies hanging from trees, streetlights, and electric poles. And even more horrifying were the crowds gathered below. There were pictures of men, women, and children, dressed in their Sunday best, with smiles on their faces and sodas in their hands, some smiling as they looked up at the hanging body.

The two women consoled each other behind the counter as I sat staring at the photos myself, transfixed and affected, as if we were watching and experiencing something together. There was a power that these visual images held over those of us looking at the violence and the crowd looking back at us through the photos. Contemporary witnesses, including myself, were mesmerized, disturbed, pained, and angry—struggling to comprehend the incomprehensible. Over and over again, in newspaper and magazine reviews and in postings on blog forums, there were questions that exemplified the shock felt by those whose understanding of racial violence in the United States had been disrupted: How could this have happened here (in America)? Who are those people and how could they do something like this? What were the purposes of these pictures? Why do we have to see these images now? What of this is still with us?

The overwhelming need to understand the incomprehensible and unrecognizable violence presented in the visual images and make sense of "how hate and fear transformed ordinary white men and women into mindless murderers and sadistic torturers" seemed an urgent matter at the time.[2] But through the eyes of one who had been working on the contemporary imagery of racial discipline in the reality crime program *COPS*, I saw something slightly different. There was a moment of recognition at the time and in the moment of that rewitnessing. I saw the photos not as documentation of irrational brutality but as modern components of a visual regime of racial violence and discipline that had a function and a purpose.

Furthermore, I saw the mediation of these photos in the form of this book as a component of the complex way in which the understanding of history works to negotiate the notions of present-day racial discipline that I recognized in the television show *COPS*. The visual reverberations of bodies whose humanity and humanness had been so viciously destroyed and consumed by the crowds, the cameras, and the viewers of the postcards, operating in the name of "justice" and upholding law, safety, and order, were to me strikingly similar, not so much in the actual form of destruction but in the moment of danger that it identified.

Compelled by Benjamin's call to seize hold of a memory in a moment of danger, this chapter looks at how *Without Sanctuary* illuminates the function of racial violence and discipline and the idea of historical progress. It historicizes the continuing practices, functions, and relations to contemporary racial violence and White Humanity's emergence as value to be protected. Here, *Without Sanctuary*, as a complex visual object, evidences the ways seeing is indicative of the continued practice of violence, discipline, and the material value of the body, as image and actualized object. As a twenty-first-century museum exhibition and an expensive photo art book, the vision of racial discipline in *Without Sanctuary* provides not just a disturbing illumination of America's dark history but an attempt at redeeming this dark past with the resurrection of the bodies through the display and respectacularization of American lynching. This resurrection imparts a form of ironic relief—ironic because *Without Sanctuary* imagines a reckoning and redemption of the past through the act of rewitnessing. However, this relief is a reprieve that exists within a present that resembles much too closely the past from which it seeks redemption.

In the same moment that debased and brutalized bodies within the photographs reappeared in *Without Sanctuary*, mass audiences were also witnessing violent racial discipline in "real time" with the television program *COPS*, which was then in its eleventh year. *COPS*, along with similar reality crime programs that quickly followed, appeared on network and cable stations, while new online streaming video technology provided an inside look at the "live" booking and jailing of people in several county jails around the country. These images of racial violence—men, women, and children chased by dogs, handcuffed with arms and legs restrained, or displayed face down, bent over the hood of police car, or held down by the heavy boot of officers pointing a 30-gauge rifle at the back of their heads in contemporary fields of vision—are horrifically close to the past images of disciplined racial bodies. Onlookers from their homes, seated in front of their televisions today, continue to sanction the practice by bearing witness and standing vigil over their own material value—White Humanity—but now do so through a discourse of enlightened humanitarianism and the ideals of racial progress and liberal equality.

From the privileged vantage point of the present and the remediation of racial violence via the book and museum exhibition, *Without Sanctuary* attempts to achieve redemption through the act of bearing witness, once again, to one of the most brutal acts of racial violence and discipline in U.S. history. This vantage point allows its new witnesses to regard their culpability and their relationship to racial discipline as a reprieve from this unfathomable past, a reprieve enabled by a convenient but false understanding of historical progress that assumes both that the brutalities of racial discipline are, in fact, over and that an enlightened humanitarianism now prevails in the United States. It is this false understanding that occludes the present conditions of racial violence and discipline and the use of the racial body in a time of crisis. Here, the twenty-first-century spectators were eager to declare dead and buried (or to resurrect as an indictment against "modern-day" lynching) the practice of lynching and public murder.

This chapter examines the ways in which the resurrection of this past and the respectacularization of racial discipline in *Without Sanctuary* as a book and museum exhibition were received and mediated by the discursive structures and institutions, spaces, and publics that attempt to construct a redemptive meaning. It is here where Benjamin's secret agreements between the past and the present can be seen in the continuity of the racial violence that serves the accumulation of capital, particularly in the form of White Humanity. The chapter traces this continuity, first, by analyzing the appearance of *Without Sanctuary* in newspaper, magazine, and journal reviews to establish the initial shock, disruption, and anxiety felt by the initial witnesses in 2001. Second, it examines the photos to see what is being seen—to look closely at what Amy Louise Wood, in *Lynching and Spectacle*, refers to as the spectacle and spectatorship—what it is that compels the crowds of the twenty-first century to once again bear witness to the incomprehensible level of banal brutality, the complicity of the crowds, the sociality and spectacular quality of the practice, and the exacting destruction of the body. Last, it examines the attempts at reconciliation and redemption through the discourses offered by the authors of *Without Sanctuary*, by the reviewers of the exhibition and book, and by the institutional leaders and academics. These discourses were propelled and enabled by the ideals of progressive humanism and liberal enlightenment as the science of both history and law is commonly understood.

The presumption that the lessons of history would lead to even further "racial" progress existed in the attempt of authors and readers alike to understand what of this violence is still with us. This examination reveals most clearly that the rewitnessing of racial discipline in *Without Sanctuary* was a missed opportunity to deal with the present situation of racial state violence as embedded in the histories of nation building through the colonial and neocolonial practices of capital acquisition and accumulation. The lessons of history are a vacant script of humanitarian progress unattached to the value of the disciplined body that leads to a public blind to its own present-day brutality, a brutality on display in *COPS* and the work of the state and capital today.

Without Sanctuary, January 2000

As the twentieth century turned and a new millennium began, *Without Sanctuary* stirred the public's consciousness, for a moment at least, by asking its witnesses to consider the history of torture, terror, and brutality in the United States. The intent of *Without Sanctuary* as a museum exhibition and book was, as Congressman John Lewis explained, to "make real the hideous crimes that were committed against humanity."³ Initially, the photos collected by Allen were deposited with the Robert W. Woodruff Library at Emory University in Atlanta. Later, Twin Palms Press in Santa Fe, New Mexico, which publishes specialty art books, published eighty-nine of the photographs along with essays by the congressman John Lewis, historian Leon Litwak, and *New Yorker* staff writer Hilton Als, as well as an essay by James Allen who annotated the book. Published in 2000 and distributed throughout the United States in both independent and major chain bookstores, the book was widely reviewed, along with the exhibition, as the reappearance of these visions disrupted the U.S. sense of itself. As *Without Sanctuary* revealed lynching as a practice so public and so extremely violent, it came as a shock to the understanding the United States had of itself and the prevailing sense of a humane and democratic identity that it embraced. The photos stood in their realism as evidence and verification of a level of brutality that had, until the photos appeared, been occluded either by mainstream accounts of racial violence against Black people during the antebellum and Reconstruction era in the South or by the idea of this violence as only existing in the South. The shock felt by those who were rewitnessing the dark history of America is testament to the transformation and change in the spectacle of racial discipline and the forgetting demanded by a desire for narrative closure.⁴

The photographs that made up the exhibition and book were part of a collection acquired by James Allen, a self-proclaimed "picker," who over the course of fifteen years excavated the lynching photos from dusty attics, dresser drawers, and old photo albums all over the country.⁵ Allen collected over 150 photos—paying up to $30,000 for one panel of photos—and approached several photography museums with his collection, including the International Center of Photography in New York, which refused the photos. Sixty of the photos later appeared in an exhibition titled *Witness: Photographs of Lynchings from the Collection of James Allen* at the Roth Horowitz Gallery in Manhattan in January 2000. The display of the photos was sparse and modest; without text or documentation, they stood on their own without explanation. The gallery was a very small space and ill-equipped to deal with the crowds and unexpected national attention that the photographs would bring. The showing at the Roth Horowitz Gallery taxed the space's resources as the venue could only hold approximately fifteen people. According to the *New York Times*, visitors waited three hours in line during the cold winter months to gain entrance. The gallery finally had to issue tickets, which it had never done before. As the crowds grew, CNN sent news correspondents, the *Today Show* televised a segment from the gallery, and the BBC and German TV also covered the exhibition. In addition, Stevie Wonder, Oprah Winfrey, and Roger Rosenblatt arranged for private tours.[6]

According to the *New York Times*, this exhibition drew enough attention to garner a showing at the New-York Historical Society that was cosponsored by the Community Service Society. *Without Sanctuary: Lynching Photography in America*, cocurated by James Allen, drew in over fifty thousand visitors in the first four months. The exhibition then traveled to the Andy Warhol Museum in Pittsburgh, in 2001, and proceeded to tour the country over the next five years. Unlike the very sparse exhibition at the Horowitz gallery, at each new venue, the photos were accompanied by additional historical accountings of lynching in the United States. The last stop for the tour was in Atlanta at the Martin Luther King Jr. National Historical Park, which was the most involved and extensive of exhibitions. The MLK Jr. National Historic Site offered a counterhistory with video documentary, placards explaining the history of lynching, and glass cases that held the anti-lynching publications of Ida B. Wells, the NAACP, the Communist Party of the United States, and the American Crusade to End Lynching. This was a much more extensive counternarrative of lynching history than that told by the photos alone at the Roth Horowitz Gallery.

From the first appearance of the photos at the Roth Horowitz Gallery in January 2000 to their present permanent housing at the Black Holocaust Museum in Milwaukee, Wisconsin, the photos have remained a startling phenomenon. *Without Sanctuary* initiated a national discussion on the dark history of terror in the United States that could be seen in the thousands of responses posted on *Without Sanctuary*'s website, on CNN and NBC News websites, and on local and national radio shows, including NPR, which produced several shows on U.S. lynching prompted by the exhibition and book.[7] Numerous magazine articles, scholarly print journals, and other internet publications clearly indicated that the discussion on the revealing of these photos was as much about the respectacularization of the bodies as it was about the reality of the past itself.

As soon as the crowds appeared at the Roth Horowitz Gallery, writers and spectators attempted to understand the public sentiments of curiosity, revulsion, horror, guilt, and loss. The initial moment of looking at the images is one of genuine shock, confusion, revulsion, and disgust at the reality of what lynching as a collective practice entailed. And, although the initial response of reviewers and commentators was overwhelmingly one of horror and disbelief, it was at the same time driven by an inability to simply look away. It is not difficult to understand the impact of photographs and the reflex to distance oneself from the images by averting one's eyes or turning away or through a statement of disavowal. The incomprehensibility and reckoning became more specific as many reviewers and visitors proclaimed their disbelief at the level of barbarity that is part of U.S. history. A writer for the Copley News Service, for example, stated:

> The media's coverage also indicates that, while many who had come to see the exhibit had known racially motivated lynching had occurred in the past, they didn't know there were so many. . . . Nor did they understand that the lynchings were often not the furtive act of the few, but communal events.[8]

Many reviews acknowledged the shock the witnesses confronted and a renewed understanding of the history of lynching exposed by the exhibition and book. Lynching in its graphic reality had become lost to those things that disappear "bad histories."

For some, it is a visceral moment too difficult to endure. As a reviewer for the Andy Warhol opening stated, "There, one horrific apparition after another makes visceral what one dares not imagine. Comprehension is also elusive."[9] The *New York Times* reviewer Brent Staples, who reviewed the exhibition held at the New-York Historical Society, explained that "most of us have witnessed things we would have been better off never having seen."[10] Staples found the exhibit beyond difficult and refused to witness the barbarity of the images. His statement is an example of how, for many, the pictures of the tortured bodies were not only beyond comprehension but, as he put it, "too perilous to suffer through." Using Susan Sontag's experience as a child with Holocaust photographs she came upon in a bookstore, and her realization that there was a limit to the amount of horror to which one is able to bear witness, Staples explains his reaction to the images:

> Like the 12-year-old Susan Sontag in that bookstore, I reached my limit quickly and left the room. I returned briefly to take some notes and was on my way never to return. There is an unbearable measure of horror here that I have no interest in learning to endure.[11]

What Staples was uninterested in enduring, whether to protect his sense of his own humanity or disassociate were images described by others as sickening, disgusting, and relentlessly horrifying. The *Village Voice* writer Cynthia Carr claims that *Without Sanctuary* "brings an art photography format to a collection of lynching pictures that are sickening to behold."[12] The *Art in America* writer Sarah Valdez exclaimed that "limp necks, shackled wrists and bare feet hovering over the ground produce a visceral horror."[13] It was a horror that Valdez acknowledged as incomprehensible, while Carr could only remark that "the photos convey a dehumanization hard to put into words."

Critics confessed to a complete inability to comprehend or analyze the histories depicted by the postcards. Valdez acknowledged the "overwhelming emotional power" of the images that produced a "rush of adrenaline brought on by viewing the lynching photographs that seems to make it impossible to think at all."[14] The book garnered no less of a reaction from Cary Clack, the book reviewer for the *San Antonio Express-News*, who tried to articulate its incomprehensibility: "My hands have closed hundreds of books after they have opened my mind and left me satisfied, perplexed or even more curious. Yet no book has so abused me and left me as speechless as has the one that lies two feet away on my desk, a book that repulses me."[15]

These forms of repulsion and denial were responses not only to the intense and involved ritual of terror—the advertisement, the mobilization of, at times, crowds of thousands of people, the actual destruction—but also to the practitioners. As much as the destroyed body is central in the photographs, it is the crowds that compel the most attention. They display the horrific and brutal murder of men, women, and children at the hands of many reviewers would call seemingly "decent everyday people," leaving witnesses frightened at their own relation and kinfolk and the idea that such horror was possible among people who appeared so normal—like themselves. In the foreword written by Congressman John Lewis, he asks, as many others have, "What is it in the human psyche that would drive a person to commit such acts of violence against their fellow citizens?" The idea that the crowds appeared to be like everyday people was a key point in the contemplation and deliberation of the photographs.

In attempting to learn who were *those people*—those that could commit such atrocities, it becomes clear that their behavior made sense, to them, only in terms of seeing the crowd as inhuman or unhuman. The border between contemporary viewers and the crowds that gathered under the bodies of the lynching victims was reified not simply in establishing the inhumanity of the gathered crowds but in their *inhumanness*. Allen begins this rendering as he states of the photos, "It was the corpse that bewildered me as much as the canine-thin faces of the pack, lingering in the woods."[16] These crowds of everyday people could not possibly be part of the humanity to which the contemporary museumgoers belonged—they became simply an inhuman mob at which museumgoers also directed their disgust and repulsion. In this cultural context, both kinds of crowds came to establish and solidify their continued place as the normative subject of humanity. Kathy Janich, a writer for the *Atlanta Journal-Constitution*, quoted a woman at a showing in Atlanta,

Georgia, as saying, "This is why we hate Hitler. We always have to remember to look at the past, to remember our inhumanity."[17]

Over and over again in reviews and comments left on the blogs, Hitler was used to reference the incomprehensible violence of the crowd's performative brutality.

But We Must Be Forced to See

The shock, repulsion, denial, and refusal to witness that occurred in response to *Without Sanctuary* became a spectacle in and of itself. The unmanageable crowds and national media coverage meant that some could not take their eyes off the images presented in the book and exhibition. The brutal spectacle depicted in these postcards was not some premodern and clandestine act of back road vigilantism as is commonly thought or presented in popular culture. These monstrous killings took place in the centers of towns and modern cities before gathered crowds of everyday citizens. They were contemporary with the great markers of modernism: while Picasso painted, Tchaikovsky composed, and Joyce wrote, crowds gathered from Ohio to Florida to watch the ritual mutilation of Black men and women. Violence in the form of defilement and complete debasement of Black bodies for the purpose of entertainment was not something unfamiliar to modern audiences, as the photographs themselves attested to how lynching existed well into the twentieth century and the modern nature of the practice.

In addition to the documentation of lynching that materialized as a photograph taken by a viewer, the photographs were also objects that participants and observers could purchase as postcards at the event and send to friends and family in the next state or on the other side of the country. These postcards were part of the material sent along the network of familial and intimate relations establishing the social and economic order of the South in the Reconstruction and post-Reconstruction eras. The brutality of lynching and the basic notion of White supremacy that it denoted aided a sense of social order at the turn of the twentieth century. The memento functions as a shocking and disturbing documentation of lynching that calls our attention to the value held by the visual display of racial violence as a form of public entertainment—a place where families and friends would gather at what was called (on the back of one postcard) the local "Negro Barbeque." The status of these postcards as objects accounts for the undeniable role of spectacle as central to the U.S. history of publicly viewing, consuming, and circulating torture and terror in the service of "justice" and "social order." They were now incomprehensible to their present-day witnesses.

One purpose of lynching is to reduce or extinguish the humanity of Black people through a perverse and complicated practice that is revealing what is at stake in the complete debasement, consumption, and eradication of the racial body. With the body as the central referent, what can be read in the images is a brutal process of debasement and defilement that is sexually charged and reliant upon the gendered maleness of the body. The liberties taken with the racial body as it is bound, stripped, beaten, dismembered, and burned to ash demonstrate the value of the spectacle of racial discipline. The majority of the lynched subjects appear to be young men with trim and muscular physiques. Almost all the photographs show a ritualistic sexual disrobing of Black males. Suspenders are taken down, and shirts are torn off. Some hang with their pants around their ankles. In every instance except one, all non-Black males remained clothed, pants on, belts secured, and shirts buttoned. The bodies also reveal, in their often complete obliteration, the value of Black life—as the hanging, shooting, dismemberment, and burning of Black bodies were rituals that required hours of preparation and labor by its practitioners. The body in the photos for the viewers of *Without Sanctuary* becomes a focal point of their contemporary relationship with the racial body that once held a social, political, and economic value in its violent death—a death that required the recognition of the community and of the public. In these detailed photographic images, the practice of racial discipline was displayed as a practice of proud and perverse exposure.

The popular distribution of photo postcards of lynching along with hair and body parts of the mob's victim was at one point a customary practice in the South as well as in the Southwest. The recipient of the postcard could look at the violent spectacle of racial discipline and recognize consent, pride, pleasure, and righteous self-regard in the expression of the crowds. The postcard images functioned, in part, to present the consummate control of White right in the South. They were a modern mimetic form of social and race relations embodied in the "strange fruit" that hung from trees and city streetlights in the twentieth century.

In this context, the images of *Without Sanctuary* suggest the centrality of the visual to racial discipline. These events need to be witnessed to serve their function. Lynching depended on the presence of crowds that would corroborate and testify both that Black humanity was not valued unless in punitive pain and, moreover, that this was a collective sentiment. The vast geographic and cultural distribution of these postcards suggests the reach and range of the social networks along which these spectacles and racial terrors carried recuperative force. Indeed, this dispersion throughout the country suggests not only the banality of the practices and the consumption of the images but a documented sense of accomplishment in the establishment (in the postwar Southwest) and reestablishment (in the Reconstruction era South and Northeast) of the social order that they evoke and in the "entertainment" they provide. Last, these images and their cultural meaning become a site for the dissection and parsing out of the operations of racial discipline and violence—to see for ourselves how debasement transpires in the racial body and transforms it from subject to object.

What is shocking about these photographs, and critical in our attempt to understand racial discipline, is the very sociality of the practice. As John Litwack explains, "No member of the crowd wore a mask, nor did anyone attempt to conceal the names of the perpetrators. . . . Reporters noted the active participation of some of the region's most prominent citizens . . . [and] the white press and public expressed its solidarity."[18] These photos document not just the brutality of lynching but its public spectacular nature and the shared collective experience of racial discipline as a righteous act. The act of bearing witness, as seen in groups as small as a handful of individuals to crowds that numbered in the tens of thousands, shows the importance of the collective features of racial discipline. Through this bearing witness en masse, the spectacle of the mutilated Black body becomes more than the pragmatic sum of punishment for a criminal act: it becomes the symbolic locus both of racial and social order and of anxiety and the accumulative value of the ideal of humanity.

Located in busy town centers amid modern buildings and modern infrastructures, the people of these cities and towns were onlookers, necessary witnesses to the practice of racial discipline. They were young and old, male and female. Crowds gathered in numbers from the hundreds to the tens of thousands in a practice that was not considered shameful or to be hidden from innocent eyes. In fact, it was an event to which fathers would take their children and wives to show their duty as chivalrous white Southern men.[19] The setting was just as often a large urban arena filled with tens of thousands of witnesses who arrived on trolley cars to an "event" lit by streetlights.

In November 1909, Will James was lynched in the city center of Cairo, Illinois. A sea of dark felt hats filled the street, as the crowd faced forward toward the brightly lit Hustler's Arch, a prominent landmark in Cairo where the city hung its banner for the annual Fourth of July Picnic and the County Fair. The streets are crisscrossed with electric cables running from telephone poles to lampposts and back again. The electric lighting, the cutting edge of modern urban design, that was fitted to the arches produced a stadium-like arena from which James was hung before being shot, mutilated, and dismembered. His burned head was later left on a tall wooden pole in the city center at Candee Park. On the right of the photo, two men in suits have climbed a telephone pole to get a closer look. In the photo, we can see that the crowd gathered in the center of Cairo numbered in the thousands to watch the spectacle. Upon closer inspection, the crowd can be seen bending over, as if peering into a well, to view James's body after the rope broke and his body landed in the middle of the street.

In many photos, the faces of those in the crowd were sometimes dour, but more often than not they were cheerful, proud, and at ease. That men were clothed in overcoats and ties, shirts tucked in, and women in dresses with their hair done makes clear that they prepared for the gruesome events. Some men are shown with arms around each other, pulling each other in toward the camera to share the accomplishment and show unity. Faces smile for the camera and bodies pose to show pride next to the horrifically mutilated corpses. They have proven to themselves and to all others who bear witness— whether onlookers on the fringes of the crowd or postcard recipients three states away—that the value of Black humanity lies in its accomplished and violent humiliation and complete debasement.

On September 28, 1919, William Brown, accused of molesting a white girl, was hung from a trolley poll and mutilated. His body was riddled with bullets and then burned. In the postcard documentation of this event, we can see a large crowd hovering over Brown's remains. As in almost every photo with a crowd gathered, men as well as women are dressed formally, as if going to dinner or to town or church on Sunday. The men pose and stand over Brown's remains, wearing overcoats, hats, gloves, and shirts with dress ties. On the left is a young man in a soldier's uniform standing in front of several young men who stretch their necks as they struggle to be included in the photograph.

The appearance of properly attired participants demonstrates that the crowd is invested in the performance of civility. The gloved hands (these are not work gloves) demonstrate a hiding of brutality—a way of maintaining a feigned distance from the brutal labor they have just engaged in. The neckties on the men remain tidy, primed, and unloosened as if both looking their best and showing pride in their accomplishment and posing as a team with a prized trophy. Along with this feigned propriety, the posturing of attainment and acquisition is a key feature in the images. An older man in the left of the frame with a bowler hat places his right leg atop the smoldering pyre where Brown's remains lay. Similarly, the man next to him sets his walking cane out in front of him as if also to lay claim to the almost unrecognizable body. They stand straight with righteous resolve and pride, looking you in the eye with a firm understanding of who they are and the meaning of the gathering.

The boastfulness of the crowd shows up on the backs of the postcards in chilling accounts of the lynching. Written on the back side of these postcards are accounts and sentiments that reveal the banality, as well as the jubilation, of racial discipline. On the back of one postcard, where the burned, legless, and armless torso of Jesse Washington hangs from a telephone pole over a crowd of men and young boys, a son writes to his mother:

This is the Barbeque we had last night. My picture is to the left with a cross over it.
    Your son, Joe[20]

On another card that displayed the body of Allen Brooks hanging from the archway in the middle of downtown Dallas, with thousands of people filling the public square, there is a carefully drawn arrow by the sender, pointing to his place in the crowd. It reads as follows:

Well, John this is a little token of a great day we had in Dallas March 3rd—I saw this on my noon hour. I was very much in the bunch. You can see the negro hanging from a telephone pole.[21]

And yet another card, with a barely discernible and unidentified headless torso hanging burned between two pine trees, reads forebodingly:

WARNING
The answer of the Anglo-Saxon race to black brutes who would attack the womanhood of the South

Without Sanctuary also contains an image of a different kind of postcard, the only one of its kind in the book with a token of the actual remains of the victim. The disturbing postcard depicts the lynching of Thomas Shipp and Abraham Smith. Their bodies hang together from a large tree. Beneath them stands a crowd of both men and women. In the center is a man pointing to the bloodied disrobed bodies. His forearm is tattooed with the bust of an Indian woman. Inscribed in pencil on the inside matting of the photo:

Bo pointn to his n**a
Klan 4th
Joplin Mo. '33

Pressed between the glass and the matte are locks of the victim's hair. Although it is the only image like this in the collection, James Allen, based on accounts from early Southern newspapers, asserts that the taking of "tokens," or the absolute consumption and acquirement of the body, was a common practice.

Why Must We See

Taking the pulse of the audience that had gathered at the Roth Horowitz exhibition, the Pulitzer Prize–winning journalist J. R. Moehringer explained that the members of the crowd would "shake Allen's hands warmly and thank him for what he had done—then ask him in the next breath why he did it."[22] Moehringer tallied the critical responses that insistently questioned the exhibition and concluded with the questions, "Was he motivated by compassion—by money? Is he a crusader—or voyeur?"[23] Allen's motivations were questioned throughout the exhibition's tour. He was repeatedly asked what compelled him to collect and present the images, as the benefits were not evident to everyone.

Even Allen and James Cameron felt that the necessity of resurrecting these images required some explanation, and they understood that what they were presenting would be troubling and confusing. Lynching in the United States was considered by many to be an act of back road vigilantism enacted by a few vehemently racist practitioners; therefore, to see it as a modern act of terror at the hands of normal everyday folks, presented in all its realism, was a shock to viewers. Allen and Cameron's intention, they said, was to reveal the truths of lynching as a preventive measure against a similar future. Allen begins the book by claiming that "*Without Sanctuary* brings to life one of the darkest and sickest periods in American history." His hope, he states, is that "*Without Sanctuary* will inspire us, the living and the yet unborn generations, to be more compassionate, loving and caring." He concludes his remarks by stating, "We must prevent anything like this from ever happening again."[24]

This was the key narrative of the collection and its display—its purpose was to face the reality of the past to prevent it from ever happening again. The Emory University president William M. Chace, after two years of debating the potential controversial outcome of exhibiting the photos, stated at the opening ceremony, "As we learn and as we teach our learning, we at times must—if we are honest—confront the terrifying. We must learn how at times people have behaved, very badly behaved. Our only comfort comes from our knowledge that people have not always behaved badly." Thee Smith, the associate professor of religion and head of the committee tasked with holding forums to gather reactions to the possibility of displaying the photos, believed after much deliberation that the exhibition "could provide the catalyst for a kind of breakthrough on race awareness in the US like nothing else has been able to do."[25]

This declaration that the repetitions of the past were preventable—if we learn from the lessons of history—relies on an assumed discontinuity with present practices of racial discipline and violence. The violence and brutality exposed by the photographs became separated in a time disconnected from the conditions of possibility from which they emerged—they are for Allen an "anything" that has the possibility of being prevented. His remarks unwittingly set up the images in a way that makes the new twenty-first-century witnesses of historical racial violence less culpable. His remarks and others like them distance the White kin relations in a way that provides an ironic relief from the disciplining of the racial body today. Repeatedly, the question of the motivation or the benefit of the resurrection of this history is reconciled with this narrative of learning and healing, that in order to have a future free of these types of atrocities we must confront our past. As Smith went on to say at the opening ceremonies:

> If you are praying pray on behalf of the victims . . . if you are a forgiving person, forgive the perpetrators for the sake of the possibility of rehabilitation. If you are a generous person, grant to the photographers the possibility of underserved grace: that their images and craft may be used for nobler causes today.[26]

The justification of the resurrection of the images lies in their power to potentially prevent future racial atrocities. This intention relies on a notion of history, as reflecting a moral trajectory of lessons learned and humanitarian progress that presumably emerges from them—a magical notion of exorcism that is to be reconciled in a collective conscience. An editorial for the Copley News Service explains that "facing history is the only way grievous wrongs can be atoned for and the lives of the innocent—past and present—redeemed."[27] In many other reviews, the idea of the lynching past is explained as an unhealed wound and a national trauma, and the resurrection and witnessing of *Without Sanctuary* is widely seen as an act of hope, a step in the process of healing history's wounds.

Although Cameron and Allen and thousands of others who rewitnessed the spectacle of *Without Sanctuary* believed that its redemptive power would heal the wounds of history and prevent "anything like this happening again," others were not so certain. The historian George Fredrickson understood how visualizing the horrors of lynching might contribute to the struggle against racism but questioned the book's effectiveness as a vehicle for promoting awareness because it could lead to misconceptions about the actual practice of lynching. And, for Fredrickson, the photos did not add significantly to an understanding of lynching; they offered only shock value that might potentially move "whites to build up some immunity to the kind of racism that still sanctions violence against Blacks."[28] This idea of ongoing racial violence and its connection to the past emerged in online commentary, message boards, and responses on radio shows that engaged *Without Sanctuary.* One reviewer explained that the inexplicable horror in *Without Sanctuary* is seen in many acts of hatred, intimidation, and racial violence:

> Today we must bring to bear our own political understanding of exclusion and oppression partly inscribed in the disturbing memories

of James Byrd Jr., Matthew Shepard and the mounting number of victims of hate crimes by lone gunmen, before and after 9/11. . . . This
means thinking about connections between lynching, the placing of
the noose in some workplaces to intimidate black employees, the string
of unsolved bombing of a gay bar, two women's health clinics and
the 1996 Olympics and the recent beating of two black brothers by
skinheads in a trendy "alternative" neighborhood.[29]

In this list of liberal tragedies to which the practice of lynching is traced,
one realizes not only the transhistorical relations of racial capital in discipline and violence but also what is at stake in the narrative framing. The atrocity of lynching and the violence is explained only through metaphor—a structure that distances present-day witnesses from the violence. It is also used
as a blanket symbol to incorporate all present-day acts of violence and hatred as one universal behavioral mishap. These responses map the connections only as an interpretation of intolerance and social prejudice that can
potentially be resolved through a humanist view of reconciliation and recognition. A continuum of injustice is grafted onto lynching that threatens to
trivialize the history of its practice in the urgent need to explain the incomprehensible horror of the act. The responses attributes it to the "evil in us all"
which erases the history of violence in relation to material investment, racial
capitalism, and liberal frames of vision. There were, however, critics of the
idea of the break with history who came closer to seeing a contemporary version of lynching.

When the first exhibit opened, the killing of Amadou Diallo had occurred
barely a year earlier, and it was clear that, for many witnesses of *Without Sanctuary*, lynching was still part of the present experience for Black people in
the United States. The response to the lessons of history was clear—the brutal
violence that injured and took the lives of Amadou Diallo, Abner Louima,
and James Byrd Jr. remained fresh in public memory and was frequently con-
jured throughout the two-year tour of *Without Sanctuary*. Their names, in
particular, were echoed over and over again as proof of the practice of modern-day lynching and that we, as a public, have yet to learn the lessons of
history.[30] Scholars such as Hazel Carby and Eric Lott replied to these "lessons of history" by pointing out the continuity between this type of racial
violence and its important connections to larger systems of terror and history. They cite well-known recent examples of racialized violence as part of
the history of the images in *Without Sanctuary*, including Louima and Diallo, who were beaten and murdered by police only a few years earlier as well
as the extralegal killing of Byrd.

In 2004, when the photos of prison torture at Abu Ghraib prison were
revealed to the public, *Without Sanctuary* was called upon once again to ex-

plain the inexplicable. In a now widely cited essay, "Regarding the Torture of Others," Susan Sontag addresses the photography of brutal torture at the hands of the state and the incomprehensible practice of documenting these acts of violence by asking how can "someone grin at the sufferings and humiliation of another human being?"[31] In her quest for an answer, she explains that the critical issue is not the verification of murder in the photographs but by the documentation of the brutal acts—"the horror of what is shown in the photographs cannot be separated from the horror that the photographs were taken—with the perpetrators posing and gloating over their helpless captives."[32] She then goes on to explain the horror of the Abu Ghraib photos as something similar to lynching photography: "If there is something comparable . . . it would be some of the photographs of black victims of lynching. . . . They [lynching photos] were souvenirs of a collective action. . . . So are the pictures of Abu Ghraib."[33] Here, the heart of racial violence is revealed in the practice of documenting torture and terror and posing with the subjects as trophy, a practice that is innately American. The viewing of the tortured and terrorized prisoners of Abu Ghraib, for Sontag, is part of the new American and frenzied need to constantly be on camera and to document everyday activities through the digital format of the camera, to display real events in real time everywhere all at once and to emulate the increasing acceptance of violence in the United States as seen in the ultraviolent virtual images in video games. This acknowledgment, although showing that the past is not over, too quickly references the similarities between lynching and Abu Ghraib, leaving the historical connection empty of the social and political material investment involved in the violent disciplining of the racial body.

Carby also addresses the photos of Abu Ghraib by invoking *Without Sanctuary* to get at an understanding of the torture and terror inflicted upon the prisoners at Abu Ghraib. She explains that what happened in Abu Ghraib prison was not something that should be so easily understood as "incomprehensible," and calls into question Sontag's misunderstanding/miseducation of the history of U.S. racial violence. She addresses Sontag's obvious incomprehension and distress at the images of the humiliated and violated Iraqi prisoners of Abu Ghraib by explaining that the debasement, torture, and terror of Brown bodies is not new and that its history can be found in the practice of lynching and the systematic (and violent) social, political, and economic exclusion of raced people. For Carby, Sontag's quick and hasty reference to lynching is "evidence that even the best educated have learned little from the history of American racialized violence."[34] Carby's response to "one of America's foremost intellectuals" is that the images (and the people in them) of Abu Ghraib are direct descendants of lynching and "material evidence of the wielding of power, of the performance of conquest over an enemy." She sees this visual imagery as a continuity of the message of domination that is found in the carefully posed bodies of the tortured and humiliated and the grinning faces of the practitioners in both sides of the historical mirror. Importantly for Carby, the naivete of Sontag is her inability to see the "line connecting Abu Ghraib, the Rodney King Video and . . . postcards of lynching." This connection for Carby is the long history of torture and terror on American soil, with Louima as a present-day example of the violent practices against the racial body as part of this continuous line that connects these practices of brutality. She explains that the violence enacted against Louima and others is nothing new for people of color and Black males in particular.

And while Carby is right, her analysis (and those like it) fails to observe that what we are witnessing in *Without Sanctuary* is not just racial violence but the *spectacle* of racial discipline—lynching was a necessarily public act that fulfilled its disciplinary function through spectacular means. Although the level of violence in the cases of Byrd, Louima, and Diallo may be comparable to the lynching depicted in the *Without Sanctuary* postcards, the analogy ends there. The killings of Byrd and Louima—and the degradation and torture of detainees at Abu Ghraib—were concealed acts of brutality that happened to come to the attention of the public and were immediately and widely condemned. By contrast, the practice of lynching in the post-Reconstruction South was both public and widely approved. The very features that rendered the images in *Without Sanctuary* so heinous to late twentieth-century viewers—their barbarism and brutality—seemed innocuously entertaining to the original consumers of these images.

So, as horrible as they were, the most notorious incidents of racial violence that marked late twentieth-century U.S. history were not comparable to the spectacle of racial discipline enacted through lynching. This does not mean, however, that spectacular forms of racial violence ended with the last public lynching of the twentieth century. On the contrary, such spectacular violence was present everywhere as the millennium drew to a close. It appeared without comment before and after the television news shows that broadcast the sad tales of James Byrd's and Abner Louima's deaths on the widely syndicated reality television show *COPS*.

4

COPS

Racial Discipline at the Turn of the Twenty-First Century

It's early evening, and a young Black man is being chased through the fields of Memphis. He is jumping over fences and brush, running toward a row of dimly lit houses. Seven men in uniforms pursue the young man with two large dogs. As he is about to reach his home, the first dog grabs hold of a pant leg and the second dog pulls him down by the back of his shirt. The young man, who appears to be about twenty years old, hits the ground hard and screams as the dogs bite into him, ripping off his shirt and tearing at his trousers.

Each of the seven men grabs ahold of the young man. The first grabs a leg, another grabs an arm, twisting it backward, while a third holds the young man's face to the ground with his foot. The dogs continue tearing at the young man's pants, stripping him to his underclothes. The men bind his hands and feet behind his back as they yell in his face, "don't you move now . . . don't move." The young man moans as the men drag him toward the front of the house. Three children walk out of the house, followed by a young Black woman. The family waits for the inevitable, dreading what is about to follow. A public audience has by now gathered to watch and be entertained by a chain of events that will alter the life of the young family forever.

This description of a young Black man in Memphis and the violence of his capture, in front of his family and the public at large, is not a documentation of a turn of the twentieth-century lynching. This is a description of an episode of *COPS* that occurred in Memphis in 1999. The uniformed men are members of the Memphis police canine unit. The crying young man pleading for leniency, like the individuals accounted for by Wells in the *Red Record* and other documentation of racial violence, is in fear of his life. And the family witnessing the capture is well aware that their future lies in the hands of the men who hold their husband and father. The viewing public, in this contemporary case, consists of the television viewers of *COPS* watching from their homes, passing another Saturday evening consuming the spectacle of the lives of Black, Brown, and poor families permanently affected by their violent incorporation into the carceral system.

These images of violence and humiliation illustrate the continuity of racial subjugation, oppression, and terror as well as a discontinuity of this spectacle and its function in the midst of state and economic shifts at the turn of the twenty-first century. This chapter demonstrates that *COPS* replicates past practices of racial discipline through the violence and dehumanization of policed populations but in complex ways that reveal the economic, political, and ideological shifts that occurred over a century and a half. The brutality of racial discipline on *COPS* depicts a twenty-first-century time of crisis and accumulation.

In *COPS*, the images of racial violence are both continuous and discontinuous with past visions of racial discipline. They are continuous in the entertainment value of disciplining bodies through the visual forms of reality that lend themselves to Taussig's epistemic murk and fictions of the real. The form of realism in *COPS* is a means of understanding "the 'authentic' nature/culture, color and class of crime, where crime lives and breeds, its exotic habits and bizarre customs as it is juxtaposed against ideals of law, rationality, and order."[1] *COPS* is, in part, ethnographic work that creates the social truths that justify this new regime of racial discipline—the spectacle and visions of modern state power through a liberal understanding of law. However, to understand the continuity as more than the literal translation of lynching, as we saw in the previous chapter, we must examine the discontinuities found in the form of the practice and the shape of the practitioners. Therefore, to see the similar brutalities in the mirror held up to history, we need to account for the refracted reflection of violence and racial discipline. This appears in *COPS* as both part of the modern punishment system that works under the guise of public safety—justice and order rationalized through a bureaucratic and professionalized transformation—and of its complex racial appearance. The spectacle of racial discipline has moved from a practice of violence at the hands of an "unofficial" or extralegal policing group—mobs—to the modern police state, and from a homogeneous racial practice to one that is heterogeneous as it is anchored in the materiality of a violence that accumulated the value of White Humanity as explained earlier.

An examination of the discontinuities within the continuity of racial violence will enable a better accounting of the shift from the overt destruction of the body in the name of racial White supremacy to the policed racial body on *COPS*. To account for this discontinuity is to show the meaningful shift and radical reorganization of disciplinary violence—not a qualitative shift but a shift in the object and objective of punishment. I argue in this chapter against a complete and literal continuity and account for the discontinuity in two critical ways. The first is the discontinuity of the representation of race on *COPS* as it is not the straightforward White on Black violence of the post-Reconstruction era or during the settlement of the Southwest. Racial representations on *COPS* are complicated: the police are not always white, and the disciplined subjects are not always Black or Brown. The second is the shift from the practice of racial discipline at the hands of mobs to the police state. Lynching and other forms of racial violence in the twentieth century was often practiced by unofficial and extralegal groups—mobs that carried out the extralegal justice against those who transgressed and endangered the security of White material value. At the turn of the twenty-first century, the disciplining of the racial body that occurs via the sanctioned modern practice of policing on *COPS* is less metaphorically lynching than a violent practice of eradication and dismantlement through technological apparatuses of the state and its invasive categorization and processes of humiliation and debasement.

The Discontinuity of Color, Race, and Racial Discipline in the Twenty-First Century

Racial violence and discipline on *COPS* are complex: the old dualities do not hold. The police are frequently Black or Brown and those subjected to their authority and disciplinary action are, importantly, often white. And while this may appear to support a simple vision of a progressive move toward structural equality, people of color represented in the police, it is of critical importance to understand that, in spite of the racial heterogeneity of the display of police power, the violence of punishment continues to have a consistent racial logic that plays itself out in the distribution of material value.

I account for this by reading race through its symbolic gesticulations, searching for how race is articulated on the bodies of the subjects of *COPS* and the geographies in which they are located. The professional neutrality of police diction and uniform renders them symbolically White, regardless of their actual skin color. At the same time, depictions of chaos, disorganization, and nakedness render the policed subjects raced. Class and poverty are now read through what the race theorist Denise da Silva explains as the knowledges of racial difference, and what she terms as the analytics of raciality, as they are produced and inscribed on the body in the locations policed in the episodes of *COPS*.[2]

For da Silva, race always signifies the body that is outside the territory of the principles and ideas of the universal and the ruling conceptions of law and justice.[3] The racial in this case is traced through transgressions that incite anxiety, fear, and loathing, as they are antithetical to normative middle-class values and the protector of those values, the bodies of the police. Out-of-control sexuality, social infractions, familial relationships wrought with violence, drug dealing, and drug addiction are rendered as the terrain of criminality and social danger. COPS makes them "reality." These representations are perceived as so real that they can be considered factual documentation of criminality and reliable portrayals of the culture from which they presumably emerge. This reality mobilizes the seeing subject and provides the evidence needed to punish the racial body or relegate it to death.

Reality and Race in the Visual Regime of the Empirical

COPS purports to give its viewers a day-in-the-life look at an average police beat. Every week, a video crew rides with police officers to document the adventures of officers from various precincts around the country. The characters divide neatly into two opposing groups: the criminals and the suspects (or, more accurately, "subjects") on one side and, on the other, police, Child Protective Services, or probation officers functioning as representatives of the state. The stories are set predominantly in working-class or working-poor inner-city neighborhoods in New York, Chicago, Indianapolis, Memphis, Los Angeles, and other major cities across the United States.

And, although COPS is considered a television crime drama with entertainment value, it has also been seen as documentation realistic enough to provide an empirical basis for law and policy. For example, James Wolcott of the New Yorker interprets the program in this way, stating:

> These aren't ordinary donut runs we are on. . . . We are thrown into the thick of hostage dramas, drive-by shootings, domestic disputes, burglaries in progress, drug buys gone bad, tottering hookers exposing their titties to passing motorists, wounded bodies. If President Clinton really wants to study the country's urban siege mentality (which has spread to the suburbs and even some rural communities), he could do worse than to watch COPS. As an ongoing sociology lesson, it's worth a dozen blue ribbon commissions.[4]

Put another way: the structure/ideals of law, science, state, and nation converge in COPS to create the criminal racial subject discursively and materially. The reliance on realism and on documentation of behavior, space, and material goods are evidence of the difference that justifies the need for management, containment, and capture.

For Wolcott, the realism of COPS is credible enough that, as he states, it should be acknowledged by the president and used to structure crime laws and policies. Just as importantly, Wolcott acknowledges COPS's sensationalism—viewers are meant to be titillated by the extreme exposure and violation of the subjects. Another social commentator, the New Republic's Charles Lane, reads COPS with a similar sense of its ethnographic value:

> I originally conceived of watching COPS as a method of familiarizing my European born wife-to-be with the diverse regional dialects, urban demography and social problems of her new homeland. . . . COPS is a marvelous acculturation tool. . . . The more time you spend with COPS, the more you get out of it. Its dramatic impact and its social scientific value are cumulative. Night after night, domestic disturbance after domestic disturbance, shooting call after shooting call, in Little Rock, Sacramento, Kansas City, Cleveland, Nashville, Miami, San Diego County—all across this great land of ours, crime and violence are an integral part of life for thousands of people.[5]

For both Wolcott and Lane, COPS, through its realism, provides both scientific credence and sensationalized pleasure. It, thus, functions as part of a larger visual regime in which the repressive possibilities of photography and film are used to document and typologize the criminal and dangerous classes and justify the expansion of prisons and jails.[6] Wolcott advises President Clinton to watch the show to understand the country's "urban siege mentality," which Wolcott claims forebodingly has now spread to the suburbs. The 1994 Violence against Women Act added a host of new criminal penalties for men who abused women. At the same time, the state began sweeping up women as well, increasingly sending women to prison and even building more prisons to accommodate them, such as California's Valley State Prison for Women, Central California Women's Facility, and the California Institution for Women. Therefore, at the height of prison building and the production of the criminal subject that the prison cages necessitated, COPS served as evidence for the need to be tough on crime and put money behind it. COPS helped justify the caging and killing of millions of Black, Brown, and poor people by the justice system in the United States.

The realism of COPS establishes the program's value for Wolcott and Lane. Even allowing for the deployment of hyperbole as a rhetorical device, the equation of a sensationalistic television program with "social science" reports by "blue ribbon commissions" can seem plausible precisely because this program appears to present an unmediated view of criminal conduct—the reality of inner-city life that it documents. The use of handheld video cameras on *COPS* enables the show to evoke the "realism" of reportage or visual documentation. The absence of voice-over narration and the seemingly candid and unscripted comments by police officers give the program an "authentic" or "realistic" quality. In addition, *COPS* follows the techniques first developed within documentary and ethnographic filmmaking, where the action proceeds at the pace of "real" time rather than the "compressed" action time of fiction films. And wittingly or unwittingly, critics like Wolcott and Lane locate themselves in the precise subject position that the creators of *COPS* imply and inscribe in their carefully constructed representation of reality. As the camera documents the lives of presumed criminals—their homes, relationships, and familial practices—it provides an inside look at the presumed culture of crime. The viewers become the critical superego and the outside judge.

Yet, the seeming "reality" of *COPS* is simultaneously illusory and unquestionably real. The program's creators carefully construct the illusion of the criminal world they purport to find with the sophisticated and strategic deployment of images and rhetorical devices that structure the representations that appear on *COPS* through production. These representations draw much of their pervasive power from the illusion that they have not been constructed at all and are, therefore, real. Wolcott and Lane misunderstand and misrepresent the sociological meanings of *COPS*, but their gullibility as viewers reveals a great deal about the show's commercial, critical, and, most importantly, ideological success. *COPS* does reveal truths about our society, but less through its presentation of "real" images of crime or criminal behavior than through its largely both hidden and successful efforts to construct an ideological and politically inflected message about the causes and consequences of crime and the practice of racial discipline.

As a mass media production, *COPS*'s documentary power relies on the modern ideals of ocularcentric reality. Our traditions of empiricism and ethnographic documentation combine with intellectual and cultural ideals of realism and authenticity to make *COPS* an important instrument of social understanding. As a political and ideological force, it provides perpetual reinforcement for a narrow range of ideas about both the causes of crime and the identities of criminals and victims. The dichotomies of good and bad and black and white are already understood as the program presumes ideas of racial difference that are structured within the social scientific understanding of culture.

The prevailing sociological and ethnographic scholarship on crime and deviancy, particularly in cities, attempts to explain that persistent poverty and deviancy are due to the cultural inclinations of the urban poor. The "culture of poverty" theory, which asserts that the poor create a culture of apathy and fatalism to cope with destitute conditions, is the key to explaining the behavior of the underclass in relation to the economic conditions in which they live.[7] Robin Kelley maintains that the problem of such empirical approaches is their reliance on a narrow concept of culture that "uses behavior and culture interchangeably," conflating the two into a framework that contributes to the construction of the underclass as "a reservoir of pathologies and bad cultural values."[8] *COPS* operates as a mechanism in the making of racial meanings and the maintenance of a social (racial) order. With its roots both in the foundation of social science and in entertainment, *COPS* functions as a diorama of the culture of crime.[9]

Twenty-First-Century Visualities of Race

The images of bodies hung from trees and lampposts across the South, in the photos of lynched Mexicans by Texas Rangers and the piles of bodies displayed at Wounded Knee, portrayed the homogeneous practice of racial punishment. The bodies of the racial violence were predominantly men of color, although women and children were also brutalized, and the crowds were overwhelmingly white men and their families. The racialized violence we see on *COPS*, on the other hand, is complex and breaks with the continuity of racialized violence at the turn of the twentieth century. The presentation of race is heterogeneous, as the police that practice acts of violence are multiracial as are the alleged suspects and the viewers at home. This complicates any simple reading of race from the surface of these images.

The existing scholarship on crime and the representations of crime and race on *COPS* have critiqued and criticized the stereotypes of Black and Latino people as the threatening criminal element in society and White people as the protectors of the state and public good.[10] However, it is a critique of a homogeneous portrayal of police (White) and criminals (Black or Brown) that overlooks the class and material relations inherent the practice of racial discipline. The extensive scholarship criticizing the racist presentation of criminality on *COPS*, and other "reality television" programming, has not accounted for the complexities of race or questioned the fluidity of the social construction of race in the new millennium. So how do ideologies of race operate in a post–civil rights and post–affirmative action era and how does the discontinuity of race in *COPS* continue to be a racial practice?

In tracing the continually racially disciplined subject in the heterogeneous terrain of *COPS*, body language and geography play a key role. Media scholars have claimed that television is central to the construction and circulation of commonsense ideas about major social issues such as race during the 1980s and 1990s.[11] And yet, the bulk of this work overlooks the complex manifestation of racial discourse during this time, as the representations on television became more diverse and complex. The representation of Blackness during the 1980s was important because the historical staging of race and representations was "a period rich with struggles, debates, and transformations in race relations, electronic media, cultural politics and economic life."[12] So, although more Black people appeared on the screen in novel roles (such as doctors and lawyers), there was an aggressive appearance of Whiteness articulated during the Reagan years through a social agenda that focused on reverse discrimination, welfare fraud, traditional values, and anti-immigration sentiment. The new right "effectively appealed to popular notions of Whiteness in opposition to blackness."[13] This appeal relied on an understanding of race grounded in middle-class discourses about "Whiteness." These understandings of race are ideological. Black and Brown representations are situated in existing material hierarchies of privilege and power based on class (middle), race (White), gender (patriarchal), and sexual (heterosexual) differences and are articulated through the sacred values of Whiteness such as individualism, private property, and family. Blackness, on the other hand, is marked, for example, by Reagan's use of his favorite figure to rally his agenda on welfare reform—the Chicago "welfare queen" (whose alleged fraud garnered $150,000 in tax-free income and who just happened to be Black). Reagan's continuous use of this unmarked image was meant to "join *law abiding* taxpayers to an unmarked but normative and idealized racial and class subject—hardworking whites."[14]

A significant moment of representation at this time the premier and overwhelming success of the *Cosby Show* and the integration of the program into the shifts in racial visuals. The show premiered in 1984 and ran until 1992 showing all the components of the home life and familial behavior of a certain secured middle *classness* that the Cosby family represented. It was accepted and embraced by American viewers without questions—the Cosbys are a middle-class family that just happens to be Black.[15] Children are sent to Ivy League colleges, dressed in designer clothes, eating family meals in an expansive dining room, and speak a standard English free of any slang or Black English assumedly obvious markers of an upper-middle-class household in New York. The Cosbys are a family household that has abided by the rules in the era of a growing police state (i.e., wars on drugs, crime) and a shrinking welfare state. They are the representation of conservative ideals that upheld and enforced a larger state project that had its own representations of Blackness on television: Willie Horton, Rodney King, and the families seen weekly on *COPS*.

These visual dichotomies operate as part of a larger conservative strategy relying on the representation of the underclass as pathological. For example, welfare reform was blamed for producing an underclass "distinguished by sedation and satisfaction of bodily pleasures, dependency, immorality, hostility, erosion of standards, loss of civic responsibility, and lack of respect for traditional values."[16] The complicated representation of race on COPS can be understood in the same manner. In the new post–civil rights/postracial era, race is rarely explicitly referenced in the program: it remains unmarked, yet the visual rhetoric tends to manifest the historical association of Black and Latino people as deviant and dangerous criminals in need of violent discipline.

In the new era of the postracial subject, discipline at the hands of the police becomes a form of race making—one that is both complicated and reaffirmed by the presentation of class on COPS. Visually, the complexity of race is mapped out through symbolic markers of the body. White destitution—the missing teeth, the ripped and dirty clothes, the trailer park—is turned into Black criminality, and Black and Brown police are rendered nearly White as they now are the purveyors and protectors of White postracial material value. The diversity of police and the policing of White people inevitably translates to criminalblackman and his necessary punishment.

The power of Whiteness lies in its unmarkedness and the capacity to appear as not constructed at all—that it appeared in law as an abstraction becoming actualized in everyday life through political and economic structures.[17] Although the role of Whiteness in the social order is substantial and does have a structural value, the marked way in which white people are racially disciplined on COPS compels us to reconsider the centrality of the *White-unmarked*. On COPS, the criminalized lower-class white people are marked, and their visibility serves to "Whiten" Black and Brown police officers while, simultaneously, racially codifying classed white suspects as Black or Brown. However, it is important to consider the way in which the racial codification of White, as the representational power of class and its modality of understanding, is at work on COPS. The practices and aesthetics of the body are a system of racial codification dense with semiotic and discursive meanings of social and racial order, where White people are racially codified through the "nature" of their *classness* or, on the other hand, the officers as the protectors of it.

On COPS, criminal White people are racially codified through the White institution of the police and against Black and/or Brown criminality. The White suspect body is inscribed with class markers such as missing teeth and incoherent speech. White people appear to live in worse conditions than Black or Latino people. Also, their bodies tend to be bared disproportionately and are more often obese compared to their Black and Brown counterparts. White males appear without shirts more often than men of color, are tattooed more, and possess more body piercings. These markers of deviancy are elaborations that primitivize and racialize White people through class inscriptions and symbols of transgression. These elaborations are critical precisely because they underscore the relationship between race and class in the late 1980s through the 1990s and 2000s and how that relationship is mediated by visual depictions of a burgeoning criminal industrial complex.[18]

Declaring that "race is the modality in which class is lived," Stuart Hall's analysis helps us understand how the theatrics of the racial codification—the Blackening up, or the Othering of White people—occurs through markers of class that take on new significance within the rise of the U.S. investment in prisons. Hall asserts that race and class are inseparable. Therefore, not only does poor mean Black and Black mean poor but more critically that policing Black people means policing the poor and the unemployed.[19] There is a performative race work on *COPS* that attempts to turn white people into Black or Brown racial Others to separate the white middle-class viewer from its transgressive reflection.[20] It is a maneuver necessary for the viewing public to distance itself from the criminal class, the deviant, the Other, regardless of its skin color. So extreme are the poverty-ridden representations of white people that *COPS* becomes and functions much like the minstrel shows of the nineteenth century, but with an elaborate realistic twist.[21] On *COPS*, the new Otherness is produced through the presentation of class that is specific to the post–civil rights and postracial era of multiculturalism. The cultural and structural shifts emerging from a deindustrialized and globalizing U.S. economy surfaced in the discourses and popular representations as a struggle with racial identifiers that fixed themselves, for a moment at least, on the markers of class. The codifiers at work here Other white people, specifically; to be "lower" class is portrayed as deviant in the social and political arena at the turn of the twenty-first century.[22]

The poor are presented in direct opposition to the bourgeois individuality of the more affluent and so the poor represent "impurity, heterogeneity, masking, protuberant, disproportion, clamor, decentered, eccentric arrangements, gaps, orifices, symbolic filth, physical needs, pleasure. . . . the lower body stratum."[23] These representations incite fear and loathing, as opposed to what presumably represents the apex of enlightened Humanity: bodily freedom, closure, the elevated (in anticipation of admiration), static, and monumental. They claim that the protocols of the body of the highest form of the Human delineate the identity of progressive rationalism itself—representing on one hand the "great age of institutionalization in the form of asylums, hospitals, schools, barracks, prisons" and characteristically embodies the "high" discourses of philosophy, statecraft, theology, law, and literature.[24]

Whiteness of Police

Representations of the police state are a foil to the social and racial order of criminality. The state, regardless of the skin color of the officer, is rendered as White. This relationship of the White police to the racialized and classed

ordering of criminality echoes an earlier social formation: what Du Bois referred to as the white wage of the South. Du Bois argued that white workers
enjoyed a "public and psychological wage" made possible by racism, which, in
turn, hampered coalitions between white and black workers. Policing—a practice that can describe both wage labor and social and cultural practices—also
provided such a wage. Slavery demanded special police "and such was made
possible and unusually effective by the presence of poor whites . . . [although]
the great planters formed proportionately quite small as a class but they had
singularly enough at their command some five million poor whites; that is
there were actually more white people to police the slaves than there were
slaves"[25] This echo of the white wage in *COPS* can be witnessed in the officers
who resemble and protect the value of Whiteness. And, in the case of the state,
it is also *what we do not see* about the officers that normalizes their position
as the protectors of the (propertied) public. On *COPS*, the universal language
of the state, the uniformity in appearance and objective position of the police,
situates the officers as the *racial* antithesis to criminality and encourages viewers to identify with this position and, in this way, come to manage the racial
and class tensions that persist within this moment of postracial capitalism.

This is clearly seen in a segment in Cleveland, Ohio. In it, two officers walk
out of their precinct station to their patrol car; one officer is a white male approximately mid- to late thirties, the other is a light-skinned black Latino officer in his early forties. The voice-over of the Latino officer explains his motivation and the enjoyment of his beat:

> I find the crime in the downtown area to be most interesting than
> out of all the other districts because you have such a variety of dif-
> ferent people from the downtown area out into the projects and in
> ethnic areas. Due to the work population in the downtown area we
> come across a lot of stolen vehicles. . . . Pursuing stolen cars that is
> one of our primary functions.

The camera is positioned in the back seat looking out the front window and
providing a side profile view of each officer's face, shoulders, and head. Both
officers are clean shaven with neatly groomed crew cuts stopping just above
their crisp dark collars. The officers are notified by their dispatcher of a suspected stolen vehicle. Posted on the dashboard next to the display panel are
identification sketches of two Black males. Next to the sketches is a 30-gauge
shotgun held upright inside a holster mounted on the passenger side of the
dashboard.

The police begin to pursue a small red two-door economy car. They turn
on the siren as the younger white officer screams at his older colleague: "Get
on it Mel. Get on it!" The high-speed chase is on: with sirens blaring, the of-

ficers shift their posture, leaning forward toward the windshield. The viewer can see three other patrol units following in tow. As the police unit gets closer to their quarry, it appears there are three or four occupants in the vehicle. The younger officer reaches his hand out to the shotgun, takes it out of the holster, and points it out the window, taking aim at the red car. He pulls it back in as he yells at his partner "come on faster Mel faster." As the red car attempts a left turn, the driver loses control, hits a road barrier head on, and crumples in the dust and debris. The young officer yells loudly, "Beautiful. Oh, beautiful." The two officers jump out of their car; the camera follows.

The younger officer reaches the car first. Placing one leg on the driver's door, he braces himself and points the shotgun directly into the driver's seat of the smoking vehicle. A Black female officer appears and rushes toward the vehicle pointing a .38 automatic handgun at the back window of the car. A thin young black man has been thrown forward into the windshield; his legs hang limply over the steering wheel. A second young Black man is pulled from the back seat by the female officer as she holds a gun directly on his back. He is bleeding, and he stands for a moment before he falls forward. She and another Black male officer stand over the young man on the ground. The officer from the first unit steps down on the back of the suspect, his shotgun aimed directly at the back of the young man's head. The female officer steps down hard on the back of the suspect's neck as she bends down to cuff his hand behind his back. All three officers pull hard on his handcuffed arm picking him up off the pavement. The officers shove him harshly into the back of one of the police units.

Another young black man is pulled from the car and dragged toward two other police cars. Three officers pull a third young Black man from the passenger seat of the red car. His body offers no resistance and hangs from the hands of the officers as they throw him to the ground. He is bleeding from his head, ears, and mouth. The officers look down at him as the pool of blood stretches out, rapidly growing larger. The older Latino officer flashes his light on the head of the bleeding man as he bends over to search his body for weapons. The pool of blood continues to grow larger as he flashes his light on him and walks away.

This violent imagery of policing is not the homogeneous images of white on Black violence from the Reconstruction South. Instead, it is a heterogeneous portrayal of state violence at the turn of the twenty-first century and a testament to the complexities of the visual significations of Black, Brown, and White, as we know them. Shifts in social, political, and economic movements have incited the fluidity of racial formations and the images of racial discipline witnessed in COPS. However, even as the racial identifier of skin color shifts and expands to encompass deviant white bodies, the material and structural understanding of racial meaning remains intact. In the preceding description, the Cleveland police force is multiracial, and, although the suspects are young Black males, it is critical to account for the handful of Black as well as several Latino officers engaged in the spectacle. It is evidence of the extent to which the criminalblackman occupies the imagination of *COPS* viewers.[26]

Race and the Disciplining of Geography

The introduction to each officer provides the viewer with a brief preface and indoctrination to the police state, as a way of becoming acquainted with police work and the motivations and tools of the police trade (the ability to reason, a sense of fairness, courage, and intuition), the target of their work ("they," "bad guys," "those kinds of people"), and who they work for (the United States, the public, the community, families and children). The information presented reflects a standard handbook with almost scripted answers—"To protect and serve," "to uphold order," or "to give back to the community." In addition, officers typically position themselves as caretakers or overseers of these policies as well as guardians of the public: "I felt it was my duty to the community or to the families and children to protect them against the bad guys." This introduction to the officers situates them not in direct opposition to the communities they patrol but in a paternalistic power dynamic where the police are protecting the security of an abstract public versus the security of the neighborhoods.

The camera documents the streets of cities all across the country from the point of view of the officers. Details are taken from the inside of the police car looking out at the working-class or working-poor areas of large metropolitan cities. The streets of poor neighborhoods are geographic visual mappings—a terrain of representation imbued with political interest. The viewer learns from each officer the technical vocabulary of policing ("perpetrator," "suspects," "alleged," "pursuit") as well as the cataloging of human social interaction ("hostage situation," "kidnapping," "domestic dispute"). Though the cities differ, the same scene often appears: the neighborhood market, Laundromat, or small strip mall where people of the neighborhood congregate. Recurring stock characters walk through these settings. There is the neighborhood dealer, the wandering woman who has left her children at home to hang with her "buddies," older (presumably) unemployed men, and small groups of children on bikes and skateboards interacting with their community.

These introductions are also significant for what is absent. The subjectivity of each officer is concealed by their speech, uniform, and badge. Rarely is specific information given regarding the officer's economic background, marital status, sexual preferences, or familial relations. Male officers seldom have facial hair and are impeccably groomed. Female officers are free of make-up and jewelry and wear their hair tightly, even severely, pulled back away from their faces. Regardless of gender, they are free of any adornment that may mark their individuality. This presents the officers as a unified system of control and rationality and, ultimately, the apex of objective authority. In *COPS*, the police are the authors of the official reports of crime and the criminal suspects in the neighborhoods they police. The rational and controlled presentation of the police ensures their accounting and reporting of the neighborhoods they patrol—they become the expert witness to the presumed criminal culture of working-class neighborhoods and public policy discourse such as welfare, Medicaid, state rehabilitation, and parole programs. This authoring establishes what Wolcott and Lane rely on as *COPS*'s social science value.

The racial/ethnic makeup of a neighborhood is rarely explicitly stated and is implied only through visuals. A segment taking place in a pre-Katrina New Orleans provides a good example. While driving through a tree-lined neighborhood, two White male officers verbally document and categorize the neighborhood and its inhabitants. As they pass a small yellow house where several young Black men sit on the porch, loud reggae music plays, and the older male officer says with authority, "Well this is the type of music *those* people play at parties." He continues: "There are just certain neighborhoods where certain activities which are so common." The men, their skin color, and their music is what marks the geography as "the problem . . . the neighborhoods where there is a lot of hanging out on the street corners or in front of homes." The other officer, younger and without sideburns, says that his beat is the most exciting, and he considers himself lucky that he is able to work in the kinds of neighborhood where there is always "the kind of people that need to be taught how to live properly."

Neighborhoods are referenced in the abstract—*those* kinds of neighborhoods, *these* kinds of families, the average male on my beat. The criminal activity commonly presented on *COPS* consists of suspected robberies, drug deals, carjackings, and assaults against property. The "bad guys" suspected of these acts are depicted as the sole cause of the deterioration of the community. "*They* would sell drugs to their own brother and sisters," says one officer. "*They* would sell their own kids for a fix."

The officers' analysis emphasizes the aberrant nature of the behavior in these ethnic neighborhoods in comparison to the normative values of society. Many officers describe their "battle" with economically motivated crimes and familial disputes as those that lead to the breakdown of social order. The suspects are portrayed as ruthless and unfeeling, with little regard for anything other than money. While discussing their routine arrests, the officers provide the viewers with an understanding of what drives the subjects/suspects in the neighborhoods they patrol, generally blaming the home and family of the alleged suspects. One officer in a Philadelphia episode states, while arresting a young Black male:

> These kids would rather be here than school. *They* see their cousins, fathers and uncles and they think why not? It is better than going to school. The thing is that *they'd* sell from their own family or steal from them. Its more dangerous out here cause when it's over money *they* don't even care if they shoot on us.

The officer presents the behavior of criminality as inherited and intergenerational. Another officer states of the debilitated buildings and families in "his" neighborhood:

> Most times these guys [referencing a father and mother arrested for selling narcotics] are so high *they* forget to even eat or change their clothes or that they have kids. I would say that most of the homes in my rounds look like this. *They* can't even take care of themselves.

The interpretation of the suspect's/subject's behavior is linked to the physical location of the "action" through this commentary. The conditions in the streets are the visual indicators of deviancy and criminality. These visuals are the backdrop for the officers' documentation, analysis, and classification of the behaviors and motivations of the communities they police. And, with the appropriation of neutral pronouns to which perceived criminal behavior and transgression is attached, a reinvented difference emerges, a geographic categorization that is grounded in the way spatial areas are understood via laws of property. As property is law in its most basic sense, it is also social in critical ways as it discursively offers a set of social symbols, stories, and meanings. As Nicolas Blomley explains, the formation of a national identity is in part a mediation on the meanings and significance of land as property as evidenced in the frontier stories of the United States.[27] Resting on John Locke's creation-myth of property, Blomley claims that property is enacted upon in material and corporeal ways where "bodies technologies and things must be enrolled and mobilized into organized and disciplined practices . . . including owners and those to be excluded." Police must enforce the laws; legal contracts must be inscribed, signed, and witnessed, and citizens must physically respect the spatial markers of property.[28]

Language

Language is a mechanism of racialization. Language works to identify the unassimilable outsider: the exotic, the alien, the degenerate, or the subaltern.

Generally, the subjects/suspects on *COPS* speak what is considered a substandard form of speech in comparison to the police state's precise institutionalized English. Latino suspects often are monolingual Spanish speakers or speak with heavy accents and are, thus, depicted as foreign aliens. Black people on the show generally speak in a Black English urban vernacular, which is considered, at least institutionally, a nonstandard form of English.[29] Along with other scholars, Hall suggests that language is the principal bearer of cultural capital and those whose speech does not conform with the prevailing standard, such as various versions of patois or Creole, are designated as in the lower rungs of the social order.[30] On *COPS*, the Black urban vernacular, slang, and extensive profanity are commonly used by the Black, Latino, and poor white policed community.

The performance of Black or other urban and poor vernacular speech is critical in creating the Othered affectable population—the suspect/subjects on *COPS*. The contemporary form of Black urban vernacular on *COPS* is not only nonstandard; it is criminalized, as it is portrayed in relation to the culture of crime that *COPS* exhibits for its viewers. It is elaboration that marks the performance of crime racially, as it is inflected with the historical baggage of past representations as well as framed in the contemporary public discourses of crime and deviancy. The exaggerated urban slang as well as the foreignness of Spanish or those with a heavily accented diction on *COPS* resonates, indulges, and gratifies a White understanding and sensibility. On *COPS*, these languages become the language of both crime and poverty.

On *COPS*, Black and Brown police officers speak without any pronounced inflection that would mark them racially or ethnically. The standardized manner of speech resonates with the historical underpinning of language ideals established in the 1800s.[31] The language that the officers use embodies this standard. For example, Black officers never use Black English or urban slang, and Latino officers have no accent and, many times, are the most demanding that Latino suspects/subjects speak English. In an Atlanta, Georgia, segment, an older Black officer has just taken the license from a young Latino man who tells the officer that he has left his insurance papers at home. The officer, not letting the young man finish his sentence, loudly for the camera says, "You will have to speak more clearly I can't understand you." "I have left them at home please." "Until I can understand what you said I can't let you go. . . . You'll have to come with me," and the officer takes the man into custody as the segment ends.

On *COPS*, then, the officers speak a standardized universal language: policing. Their motivations, decisions, and actions can be explained through "handbook speak." Officers exist on *COPS* interchangeably; all, regardless of their geographic location, speak the same way, with the same language and the same enunciation. The only officers that deter from normative speech on occasion are in segments that take place in the South (i.e., Kentucky and Florida). More importantly, the language of policing is one that is produced by the state and understood to be not just standard English but the rational authoritative nomenclature of institutional and state power.

In addition, this universal speech renders the police as an ahistorical subject that is detached from subjectivity. Officers exist separate from a location of personal individuality. Their speaking patterns and enunciations are tethered only to the highly regulated and regimented institution of policing. This rendition acutely contrasts the "irrational" subjective position of the alleged suspects, and their homes and communities, who are marked by their geographic localities and cultural practices. The introduction to each segment— the officers informing viewers of the location and human cultural geography of the neighborhood being policed, which summons the viewer into the subject position of the officer—is repetitive and scripted and in a highly enunciated speech that is an indication of their legitimacy and their alignment with power.

The show repeats this lesson across states and geographies. In a two-part program taking place in Los Angeles, a Latino and Black officer pull over a young Black man and woman for a dim headlight. The Latino officer requests the young man's license and vehicle registration. The young man explains to the officer that he does not have the registration in the car with him but that the vehicle is in fact registered. The officer states that he could not understand him and if he could please repeat himself. Again, the young man explains and the officer looking at his partner says loudly, "Look I can't seem to understand you . . . maybe you can?" The other officer smiles and shakes his head as the first officer writes a ticket and sends the young man on his way.

Important to the language or speech of the White suspect/subject on COPS is the way in which the show racializes phenotypical imagery. White suspects speak in a manner that works to distance the middle-class White viewer from the working-poor or poor White characters on COPS. Typically, COPS focuses on the poorest neighborhoods across the country, and the White people that appear as suspects are portrayed as not only poor but destitute. Poor White people more often than their Black and Brown counterparts are unintelligible as their speech is scattered and incoherent. In one segment taking place in Wyoming, a middle-aged White woman is pulled over for an unregistered vehicle. Looking forward, she is explaining to the officer that she has not had the money to pay to register the vehicle and asks him to give her a break. He looks at her and then slightly mugs for the camera with an exaggerated look of comedic dismissal and says, "Ma'am I can't understand a word you are saying." She explains over again her predicament as he interrupts her to say, "Honey, could you please look at me when I'm talking to you." She hesitantly looks toward him and again tries to explain her situation. She is missing several of her front teeth, and he exclaims in a mocking tone toward the camera, "Whoa darlin, no wonder I couldn't understand you." She looks down at her feet as he writes her a ticket and leaves.

This is a striking and notable difference between poor Black, Latino, and white people. Many white people, as compared to their Black and Brown counterparts, are presented without teeth, impairing their ability to articulate properly. In addition, the vocabulary of White people on *COPS* is severely limited, seemingly more so than that of Black and Brown subject/suspects. A Latino and white officer answering a domestic dispute call in Houston, Texas, pull up to a small white house with broken windows and piles of furniture, boxes, and old household appliances filling their porch. An older white man opens the door and says something to the officers that the camera is unable to pick up. The Latino officer asks, "Exactly what is the problem here?" The man answers again louder this time but no more intelligibly. Suddenly, a young man and two teenage girls appear and push their way past the older gentleman who is presumed to be either the father or grandfather to the family. Each family member tries to explain to the officers what occurred earlier that evening. The officers repeat over and over again that they cannot understand any of them. As the young man becomes clearly more upset, the white officer takes him aside and tries to get the full story from him. The young man begins to explain that his sister's boyfriend had made advances to the other sister. The young man's speech is so incomprehensible that, halfway through his explanation, English subtitles appear at the bottom of the screen in order to make his English understandable to the viewing audience.

The deterioration of the White body and the inability to speak coherently distance the public viewer from poor white people and from poverty itself. The compromised integrity of the body—the missing parts and pieces and the inability to maintain a language that pairs with their Whiteness—signifies an almost defecting and defiant subversion or act of treason against the prevailing norms of liberal social mobility, an act that is inexplicable in relation to their identity as white poverty lacks a popular justification of historical structural inequality that might explain their lack of mobility.

The Discontinuity of Practitioner:
From Mobs to the Police State

As in the photos of *Without Sanctuary*, the body in *COPS* is the central referent. The bodies of the suspects are inscribed with the transgressive symbols of society's norms and ideals. The transgressive symbols are critical in explaining how violence is not only sanctioned but enjoyed. The speech, motion, and costume of the bodies convey the overdetermined—already understood—

social positions of the transgressor, deviant, and criminal and those that are conventional, normative, and legal. The narrative of *COPS* relies on the repetitive characterizations of the transgression—soiled, torn, worn clothing, cluttered, unkempt, improvised homes that are an affront to convention and bourgeois sensibilities and bodies that appear flailing, exposed, overfed, or malnourished. In their exclamations and expressions of grief, rage, and fear, they embody Stallybrass and Whites' logic of the grotesque. These transgressions are presented to evoke feelings of righteousness, resolve, and pleasure in the viewer through the twenty-first-century violent and humiliating practice of racial discipline.

It is also within and on the body of the state that rational order and sanctioned violence is understood. In direct contrast to the suspects, the bodies of the police are presented as orderly, ungendered, and physically powerful. They are portrayed as uniform, free of subjectivity, unfragmented, and impenetrable. The image of authority and objectivity can be located in their appearance, which suggests an immaculate rationality where individual race, gender, and class difference is subordinated to the uniformed universal, where the language of the state is policing. Portrayed as unbiased, police are state identified first; any indicator of bias is rendered universal by the uniform that prevents entry into their private individual person. The uniform encodes them with a rational institutional authority and an agenda that is to protect and serve the public, with badges as institutional emblems of the geographic terrain they regulate.

The technological apparatuses, including guns, batons, handcuffs, mace, Kevlar vests, military boots, helicopters, and surveillance computers, are signifiers of modern institutional scientific power. These tools are symbolic of the power the state has to often violently control, contain, and penetrate the neighborhoods, homes, and bodies of the suspected. These tools of power and penetration are a part of the larger scenario of reality and racial discipline. They are implements that have been rationalized to the work so crudely handled a century earlier. Gone are the ropes, leather straps, and rough and heavy chains; in their place are titanium handcuffs, militarized choke holds, infrared cameras, ballistic shields, and Taser guns.

These tools are the instruments commonly used to exert rationalized and sanctioned violence—of which, humiliation and submission are immediately evident—on the bodies of the suspected. *COPS* is replete with positions of domination and subjection, as in almost every segment Black, Brown, and poor men kneel in handcuffs before teasing and mocking officers. Suspects are stripped of clothing or held face down on the hoods of police cars while officers demand they assume a spread-eagle position. Such bodily submission conveys a sense of what John Langley sees as a win for the good. In an interview with a *Court TV* online magazine, Langley described *COPS* as an existential variety show about "crime and punishment, good and bad."[32] Langley's win for the good guys (versus their moral opposites) is truly an act of racial discipline as spectacle.

The symbolic representation of humiliation and debasement are violent practices that are not only classed but gendered in their performance and reinstatement of the racial and social order. To see the gendered way in which these visuals work will enable a better understanding of how the practices of discipline themselves are productive of race as in both form and content. *COPS* produces an understanding of race that is gendered and sexually charged. The camera offers a sexual angle of submission as it lingers over the backside of the suspect that is one of pending penetration. Cuffed hands resting on the lower back of the vulnerable suspect evoke sexual domination. This metaphoric arrangement of the body into a position of sexual submission takes on the manner of emasculation through its suggestions of sodomy and submission. A sense of submission and domination is evoked as men are stripped of their clothing, forced to their knees, handcuffed, suspended over the hood of an automobile, or forced face down on the ground. Exposed backs and posteriors are the visual expressions of submission and acceptance in relation to the violent and humiliating practices of the state, which is metaphorically rendered male. And suspects are, therefore, rendered as female in relation to the male position of the state.[33] The focus on the shining handcuffs that bind the suspect's dark hands, with officers hovering over them, is heavy (both literally and figuratively) with phallic symbols of technology, which titillate through desire and fear.

Stripped

The unprotected naked limbs, the torso of males, and the exposed breasts of women evoke a sense of shame, danger, and titillation as common symbols of the suspected body. The exposed body is one vulnerable to state power, without the agency to protect itself against invading outside elements. To be stripped bare or partially bare is to be situated in a position primed for a penetrable gaze or body. Images of bare chests, backs, and posteriors issue a sexually charged invitation to the viewer—an invitation to dominate and discipline the submissive body of the suspects.

Face Down on the Ground

Commonly, after a suspect is apprehended, whether after a chase or at a simple traffic stop, the suspect is asked to assume "the position" of lying face down on the ground with legs spread. With or (often) without provocation, the subject is pushed or thrown roughly to the ground. The camera keeps its focus on the back of the suspect, presenting it as an offering of submission. The individual becomes less human, as they are now a faceless subject, with the feature that individualizes humanity rendered blank. In a segment taking place in Tampa, Florida, one white and one Black officer answering a disturbance call pull up to a small house where two women and two men are standing outside. The white female officer asks what has happened, and, as the young woman explains, there had been a party, and someone had shot a gun. The officer says to the young man with dreadlocks, "Don't I know you?" "No Ma'am." The office steps in closer to the young man's face and asks him to step over to the car. He claims he has not done anything and backs away from the officer. She quickly grabs his right arm in an attempt to twist it behind his back as he resists her. The other officer then grabs the shoulder and left arm of the young man, pushing him hard toward the car. The young man continues to resist, exclaiming he has done nothing wrong. Both officers struggle with the young man, grabbing at his head and neck. The camera centers in on the boy's clothing—his low-hanging pants and polka-dot boxer shorts are surveyed by the camera. The male officer harshly kicks the boy's legs out from under him and he crashes face first onto the pavement. As a female officer stands with one foot on the back of the young man, the male officer cuffs both his hands and feet behind his back, then steps down hard on the back of his neck as the boy continues to struggle, yelling loudly that he did nothing wrong. The camera again focuses on the back of the young man this time, panning down to his wrists that are bound by the shining handcuffs. The female officer motions her gun toward the other and tells him to get face down on the ground. He lies down next to the first boy with his hands behind his back. The officer steps on the second boy's back pointing the gun directly at his head. Again, the camera pans down, centering on the second boy's cuffed wrists and dark hands and then pulls back. The segment ends.

The first boy is a commonly occurring character type on COPS, as his resistance is not about the arrest itself (because he is not being arrested for anything) but the implication of his preconceived guilt. He is resisting the imposition of guilt, the presupposition of being a criminal (i.e., for standing there, for being Black). The resistance here stems from a sense of himself as a person first—not a They or Them, in summation already guilty. And the response is standard: a swift, harsh, and violent performance of humiliation and debasement that is sexually charged and volatile. The continuous focus on bound hands and exposed posteriors from a penetrating camera angle establishes the position of power that is at the expense of the subject's masculinity. These sexually charged images are also what gives COPS its entertainment value and is an integral part of the excitement COPS elicits. The domination exercised by officers and the penetrating work of the camera collude to present a sexually submitted and emasculated subject. Sexual domination and racial domination are not separate, as bell hooks explains, and the merging of [hetero]sexuality with male domination is synonymous with the ability to assert power over another through acts of violence and terrorism.[34] In much the same way that pornographic films and videos rely on the forward movement of the camera and its centering of penetration, *COPS* centers the moment of submission with its repetitive focus on the bound body, especially the hands and feet and its lingering looks at the subject's posterior.

Penetrating the Home

One episode of COPS opens in Cleveland, Ohio. Two white male police officers are executing a search warrant with two backup units. They introduce themselves to the camera (and viewers around the country). As they explain the need for a backup unit, they begin to lay out a visual geographic map of their beat (i.e., the neighborhood they police). The camera is situated behind a young officer in his mid-thirties with impeccably groomed blond hair. He explains that a backup unit is necessary due to the reputation of the neighborhood and the possibility of danger. The camera looks out through the windshield of the police car and pans the neighborhood. It is tree lined, with large homes and dilapidated turn of the century mercantile buildings. The camera pauses and holds its gaze and surveys the front of a neighborhood market with a hand-painted sign, as three young Black men stand in front conversing.

The first officer explains to the camera, "Uh the area is known for high drug activity, always a lot of people hanging on the corner in the neighborhood. It's raining, we're not sure if there will be a lot of them out there but we are taking sufficient manpower to cover anybody on the outside." The second officer responds by saying, "There's a Jamaican store up the street that uh we have tried to hit up a couple of times, it's known for a lot of drug activity and weapons violations." The first officer further justifies the extra police by giving specific examples of the second officer's claims: "There was a time not too long ago that we were having so much trouble there at that particular store that they wouldn't let one two-man car go there alone. Whenever one went they had to send another any time there was an assignment on that general area. Just because a lot of things that leaked out about threats on policemen and a lot of weapons floating around those people that were hangings around the store."

This dialogue maps out for the viewer the racialized space of the neighborhood in which the police conduct their day-to-day work. In this instance, the officers label and categorize the streets and community spaces as Jamaican, as the camera establishes the visual meaning of the identification. The witnesses and viewers are introduced to the neighborhood's behaviors and practices that endanger the lives of the officers. The officers inform the viewer that this is a place of danger, corruption, and violence caused—undoubtedly—by the types of men that have gathered in front of the market. It is a location with which, in their words, the police have a perpetual problem: "These" types of spaces and "Those" (Jamaican) people, the abstract pronouns substantiated by the work of the camera, which continues the work of creating order and maintaining the distance between the observer and the subjects/suspects.

The officers, with two other units in tow, pull up to a home where they plan to serve a warrant. Eight male officers walk up to the front door. Four officers are dressed in everyday clothes but also sport bulletproof Kevlar vests. Each holds onto a five-foot-long steel battering ram, which they use to break through the front door of the home. One officer yells: "Police! Search warrant." The door crashes open and the camera follows the officers quickly into the home. The uncut shot follows the officers as they charge through a short dark hallway screaming "Police. Get down. Down. Get down." Over the sound of the officers, children are heard screaming and crying from all directions. The camera points down at one young Black girl as she says, "I want my daddy." The camera scrambles, turning to the left and turning to the right in an attempt to document all the activity at once as the eight officers scatter throughout the house.

The shot continues uncut and takes the viewer into the living room. Three adults are handcuffed. Two women are laid face down on the floor in the living room, hands cuffed behind their backs. One woman wears shorts and a tee shirt, while the other is in her nightclothes. Their faces are never seen throughout the entire segment. On the other side of the living room, another woman is pinned face down next to a man. One young girl with short tight braids and colorful clips sits down next to the man crying, saying, "Daddy, daddy." Her face is blurred by the camera.

The camera cuts to another set of officers who explain that they are searching for drugs. Several children run through the house. A young girl, maybe five years old, is crying hard as the main officer bends over her and tells her to stop crying. Several of the officers walk into rooms with their guns drawn. The camera cuts back to the living room and points down on the male suspect's/subject's back, focusing on the handcuffs as they shine against the dark skin of the suspect's hands.

The cuffed hands of the suspect/subject produce a sense of reassurance to the viewer by presenting the work of the state as control over the disorder of the socially catastrophic space of working-poor communities. The presentation of dominance over the alleged criminal works to address the growing concern and anxiety surrounding the moral panic of crime and legitimates the overspending of federal, state, and local money on police protection and enforcement. The suspect's/subject's presumed admission of guilt regarding his parole substantiates for the viewer not only that this man is, in fact, a criminal but also that a criminal justice system that releases its subjects too early is a faulty one.

Bedrooms are surveyed as the camera pans across rooms filled with unmade beds, candy wrappers, dirty clothes, upturned bicycles, and broken toys. It pauses on a wall scribbled with children's drawings and graffiti. A tall blond police officer in a full Kevlar vest lifts up a woman's purse and turns it upside down. Its contents fall to the floor, and the camera zooms in on the owner's personal belongings. Old drugstore makeup, including mascara and a broken eye shadow case, tampons, a small broken comb, pieces of crumpled paper, and hairpins are spread out onto the stained-carpet floor. The inexpensive makeup, broken comb, crumpled papers, and candy wrappers, reveal the personal habits and practices of the woman who presides over the home. These private belongings are displayed to the viewer and focused on as the viewer is to consider her personal practices, including her grooming habits, her age, her organizational skills, and her consumer abilities. What is accounted for here is not her criminal activity per se but the "criminality" of her ethics and behavior. The disarray of her very private belongings, such as her broken and inexpensive drugstore makeup, speak to who and what she is in an era of conspicuous consumption. Her commodities offer proof to the viewers that her habits and, therefore, her family's are less than adequate or orderly and that, most importantly, they are not the habits of the imagined proper middle-class U.S. family.[35]

The camera then focuses on beds that the officers have overturned, exposing the urine-stained mattresses of the children's beds. Unmatched thin cotton sheets are thrown back, and half-empty closets are searched. Two guns and a sawed-off shotgun are found in a hallway closet. The camera focuses on the officer who seems to be in charge of the operation. A tall blond male in his early forties explains to the audience the conditions under which he is making the arrest and the reason for his team taking extreme precautionary actions. The camera surveys the weapons now laid out on the kitchen table as the officer, obviously nervous and breathing heavily, states, "You never know about houses like these . . . always got so many people you can't watch everyone, lots of times they'll come out with a gun, and it only takes a second." The shot continues without a cut and follows the searching officers as they find one more gun and one rolled joint of marijuana. The camera again pans over the weapons laid out on the table and comes to rest on the suspect/subject now cuffed and propped up against the sofa. He faces forward sitting on the floor. "They just don't know they just don't get it," the officer mumbles as he approaches the suspect.

His explanation presents "these" people as unable to determine right from wrong or logically understand the proper way to conduct themselves in order to live and uphold the ideal narrative of domestic tranquility and civic responsibility. In the officer's narrative to the viewer about "these" types of houses, the ones filled with people of color that "always have so many people in them," the officer echoes and supports the strategic rhetoric of the conservative political agenda of the right as well as the academic findings of social scientists that back this agenda.

Political and academic reports of broken homes, absent fathers, and out-of-control fertility (and sexuality) of women of color (particularly Mexican and Black) are age old and yet brand new again. In the work of scholars attempting to understand the deterioration of social life, in the United States, and in the agendas of policymakers and politicians, families have been considered to be the critical element in the making of a strong and moral nation. In the mid-1960s, Daniel Moynihan's report, *The Negro Family: The Case for National Action*, contended that households headed by a Black female were a "tangle of pathology" at the center of the inevitable entrenchment of poverty for Black people in the United States.[36]

Subsequent research done on families of the poor are often interchangeable with the conclusions of Moynihan. Judith Stacey claims that research conducted by conservative as well as liberal think tanks asserts the belief that the prime family is made up of a heterosexual married couple and their biological children and that this construct is foundational to the welfare of children and, therefore, the welfare of society.[37] However, the contention that the normalized heterosexual family is productive of a better society took a step backward as *The Bell Curve* reclaimed old theories of nineteenth-century eugenics, claiming the innate inferiority of Black people as well as other minorities was exhibited in the biological structure of the Black Family. This research, like Moynihan's, enabled neoconservatives "to blame the disasters that their policies have brought to communities of color on the alleged inferiority of minorities themselves."[38] In the case of criminality in particular, James Q. Wilson has claimed that, although the structural discriminatory policies such as racial profiling exist, family culture remains.

The segment continues with three officers standing in the living room in a dialogue regarding what they have found. One officer stands over the suspect/subject and begins to question him as the camera is positioned at his side. Looking down, the officer yells loudly, "How come you keep these guns around with all these kids around. Doesn't seem very smart?" The suspect mumbles back, but what he says is unclear, and he speaks downward into his lap. His daughter sits next to him holding on to his arm as the interrogation continues. The suspect/subject averts his eyes, continuing to look downward, lifting his eyes to the camera for a brief moment, almost as if to see if it is still there.

The officer's assessment and explication of the situation categorizes and labels this home as a site where violence and disregard for the values of order and safety is prevalent. The focus on the guns elicits a sense of the extent to which "these" people are an extreme danger to themselves and to the public. Guns and the use of them are not only a common occurrence on television; they are also historically central to entertainment in television. However, the homes of Black people and the poor have historically different meanings. Important here is the representation of the young girl and the other children juxtaposed against the guns or drugs. The guns and drugs are implicitly scripted as the natural inheritance of the suspect's/subject's offspring.

Next, the officer asks loudly, "So have you ever been arrested before? You better tell me cause I'm going to find out." The suspect/subject mumbles again. Again loudly, the officer says, "For what? For what?" The suspect/subject mumbles again. "You convicted?" the officer asks. The suspect/subject mumbles again as the camera catches the tail end of his sentence " . . . on probation." The officer states, "So you're a convicted felon and you got possession of firearms. You're under arrest, OK?" The officer concludes his assessment of the situation, substantiating for the viewer that this is not the first time the subject/suspect has been arrested and convicted of a crime. The officer verifies for the viewer the suspect's/subject's guilt as well as both of their positions in the prevailing narrative of crime. The subject/suspect is seen as a perpetual criminal, simply unable to stay away from drugs and criminal activity. This "inability" appears to have been assisted by a too lenient justice system, one that has failed by permitting the parole of a convicted felon too early. This imagery replicates the parable of Willie Horton, which worked toward convincing the nation that criminals could not be reformed and that what society needed was stricter sentencing and tougher crime laws that would prohibit the release of its subjects.

A segment in Sacramento, California, begins with a radio call to a young Latino deputy sheriff on his night shift, regarding a stabbing. The camera is positioned in the passenger seat of the police car, facing the officer. The camera focuses in on the officer's profile from his shoulders up. He is light skinned, clean shaven, with his hair cut short, barely touching the collar. He sits upright as he drives along the streets of south Sacramento, telling the viewers that he is familiar with the home that he has been directed to and explains, "We've been to this house in the last month, I would say about ten times. They got a constant problem there. . . . They got like seven kids ranging from about seven to about three months." The camera turns toward the streets, looking out the window, and the police unit drives toward the site of the alleged incident. Headlights show dented and abandoned cars lining the streets as well as shiny new sedans. As the car pulls up to the driveway, a police unit and paramedics are waiting; from behind, the camera follows the officer into the house. A short Mexican woman directs the officer into a bedroom where the officer explains that the call was regarding a stab victim who we learn is lying on the bed with a small wound slightly bleeding.

The camera moves from behind the officer to a direct shot of a small dark woman wearing a large black T-shirt. Her hair's dark roots are a stark contrast to the blond ends, and her makeup is smudged and running down her face as the camera focuses in on her shirt, which displays a picture of Jesus Christ and two lowriders. She holds a dark-haired baby in her arms. The camera then moves into the bedroom, shot uncut over the shoulders of several paramedics and other officers as they stand over a large Mexican male, shirtless and in his mid-twenties with his arms stretched out. The officer's flashlights highlight the knife wound as the camera focuses in, moving to a tattoo of a crucifix on the suspect's left forearm. It then scans the rest of the room, surveying windows curtained with thin bedsheets, toys and clothes cluttering the floor. There are two baby cribs in the corner filled with clothes and diapers. The flashlight moves around the room and the camera follows focusing on a large shiny crucifix and then family pictures. One officer yells the suspect's name, as the camera moves back over to the man lying on the bed, "Arturo . . . hey wake up man . . . who did this to you?" He shouts again, "Arturo." The officer asks the woman if Arturo is on any drugs. She says no. The main officer informs the paramedics that he is familiar with the suspect and he is just passed out from alcohol; he is just an alcoholic. The camera cuts back into the living room where one officer tells another that he got a statement from the stabbed victim who said that he was walking home when a Black guy came up and stabbed him. One officer states, "I guess they were over there drinking (referencing a neighbor's home) . . . she pulled a neighbor to the side and said, 'hey he's always drinking and abusing me and stuff can I stay over here tonight' then fifteen minutes later we pull up and he is stabbed." Another officer states, "She was the one that probably stuck him . . . have you looked around to find a knife or anything?"

The camera cuts back to inside the home with a shot over the kitchen table. The officer's flashlight scans the kitchen table covered with dirty dishes and focuses in on a knife. The voice of an officer is heard, "You still sniffing glue, Helen?" The camera moves, scanning the walls with photos of children of various ages and two religious icons; it moves from the table to the small dark woman standing in her living room holding her baby. "No, I'm not," Helen says. The camera moves back and forth from the officer to the woman. "How come it smells so strong in here Helen . . . what's that smell?" "I don't know," she replies. The camera focuses on the woman again. Pointing downward, the officer states, "Come on . . . I've only been in here a few minutes, and I am already getting high just standing here. Tell me Helen. Look at me. I said look at me." He commands. He stares into her eyes looking for signs of inhalants. The woman begins to cry. "Either you tell me the truth and where the stuff is or you remember our little chat yesterday?" The officer threatens. "Yeah, my kids will get taken away. . . . I didn't have anything to do with it," she says. "Why does it smell like this? You do know and you give me an answer right now, were you sniffing the stuff?" he raises his voice and is now yelling at her. "No not today, yesterday," she mumbles, "I'll show you." She walks toward the bedroom. The camera follows from behind the officer.

As the camera follows the officer and Helen, it turns into a bedroom where two other officers have gathered together the older children. Six children sit on a mattress placed on the floor. Some of the children are in diapers; others are dressed in pajamas and small sweatpants. Four dark-skinned boys and two girls stare into the camera as it passes by them looking down. One of the older boys, approximately five, is told by one of the officers to help his younger brother put his pants on as the youngest boy is sitting and crying, dressed only in a diaper. The camera cuts to an officer walking into another bedroom as Helen digs a spray can of gold spray paint out of a clothes hamper. The officer pulls out several more cans hidden under dirty clothes and several boxes of Budweiser. The camera cuts to two officers talking to one another in the living room: "You know what uh . . . uh we could go with the child endangerment thing too. There's no food anywhere." The camera cuts to the main officer looking through the bedroom. It follows the officer's flashlight focusing in on a baby crib; he pulls back a small blanket and reveals another spray can. The camera zooms into the baby crib and shows yet another spray can. As the camera continues to follow the officer's flashlight, he states to the viewer, "And all seven kids sleep in the room with their mother. There are hardly any blankets." The camera cuts to the children in the bedroom, where the camera and large lights beam down. The officer asks the oldest boy again to help dress his younger brothers and sisters. They scramble through the room looking for pants and shirts. There is a urine-stained mattress on the floor and overturned furniture. The camera focuses in on a broken toy in the corner.

As the camera moves again out to the living room, one officer says to another, "Did you see the spray droppings all over the door and the crib?" The camera moves to the kitchen as it scans the stovetop covered with burnt food and dirty dishes. There are several pots filled with rotting food and others filled with empty ketchup containers and a half-empty glass. Counters are piled high with dishes covered with food, broken toys, and overturned milk containers. The camera cuts back to the living room, again positioning itself at the officer's shoulder. It points down at the woman who is now sitting on a torn chair. Four officers stand in a circle around Helen and are trying to remove an infant from her arms. She is crying and begging the officers to call someone to be with her, "I won't do it anymore just call someone from social services to stay with me. Please don't take my babies!" she screams. The camera moves down and to the left and focuses in on each child as they pass by her, guided out to the police cars by the other officers. They turn and look at their crying mother, pausing, scared and frightened. Helen grabs one of the smallest one's hands and holds on tightly, "You can't take my babies, you can't!" she screams as the officer walking the children out of the house pries her fingers off the wrist of the little boy. Helen is still holding the infant in her arms as the camera moves back up to show all four officers grab a wrist and her other arm. One officer grabs the back of her head as they take the baby from her right arm as she continues to scream.

The camera cuts to a shot outside the house with three officers taking the children out to the patrol cars. It focuses in on the children clinging to the officers, and one officer consoling them. One officer picks up one of the young boys and says, "Don't cry." The sound of babies crying plays over a cut of Helen being led out of the house by an officer, handcuffed arms held back. The camera cuts to the six children in the back of the patrol car focusing in close on their faces. Older brothers hold on to younger siblings, sisters are squeezed in between in the back of the patrol car, and some of the younger children sit on the laps of older brothers and sisters. They look directly into the camera, some with dark eyes filled with tears. The camera focuses in on their faces as the voices of officers dialogue back and forth: "Probably the best thing that ever happened to them." "I can't believe she did this to her kids man."

The camera then cuts to the main officer back in the home as both she and the camera scan the kitchen and bedrooms. The camera is positioned in front of him as he walks through the house using his flashlight as a pointing device. He explains the conditions under which they made the arrest, although he does not explicitly name or explain what the arrestable offense was. He states to the camera, "We got seven kids in a two-bedroom house. All the kids stay in one bedroom and the mother and father stay in another. After the first fifteen to twenty minutes of being in this house all the officers got lightheaded and dizzy." He opens the refrigerator. There is an empty Kentucky Fried Chicken box and can of soda. He says, "Here's the refrigerator. This is what you got for food. That's what we got for seven kids." He walks out the back door to the driveway pointing the flashlight at the garbage can. The camera points down as he lifts the lid, it overflows with empty cases of Budweiser. There is no other garbage present, and the boxes look almost suspiciously uncluttered, "Here you go. They got no money for food but yet I can count out. One . . . two. Three. Four. Five cases. I asked the kids earlier if they've eaten. A couple said yes . . . they ate some beans." The camera now points directly at the officer, the lights shine on him as he continues his explanation, "The other kids said 'no they haven't eaten today.' They will be taken to a receiving center. The baby will go to the Med Center. They'll be taken there then at that point, they'll to. . . . tell you the truth; the way it goes, they'll probably be given back to their parents. You see all this stuff. We see it every day and within a day or two they'll probably be given back to their parents. And they wonder why these kids end up dead." The camera cuts to a patrol car driving off as the segment ends.

The figure of the incompetent and deficient mother is a recurring theme on *COPS*. The behavior and parenting practices of women of color are narrated as deviant and as the cause of inner-city crime. Poverty is racialized precisely because it is gendered within the idea of the nuclear family as a normative ideal, and the family unit is a key technology in the construction of race. However, the representation of these women is portrayed as a standard of all inner-city mothers as it is taken out of context and situated in the constructed context to which *COPS* exhibits its subjects/suspects. Women of color appear unable to control their sexuality and, therefore, their fertility, affirming the ideals of welfare reformists who profess that "these" women have babies one after the other. When we are shown images of a mother allowing her children to live in an unclean and poorly furnished home, where guns and drugs abound but the refrigerator is empty, the implicit message is that the state must intervene. This representation is contradictory to the norms of motherhood and family, which are commonly portrayed as white and middle class. *COPS* portrays mothers of the working-poor and working-class communities against these ideals. Thus, they are pathologized by the media, politicians, and scholars.

CONCLUSION

The Serpent in the Garden

This work has argued both that spectacular racial violence and the visual representation of practices of racial discipline at the turn of the twenty-first century are continuous with the horrifying violence enacted against racial subjects at the turn of the twentieth century and that both were enlisted in projects spurred by moments of crisis and accumulation. Focusing on *Without Sanctuary* and *COPS* as visual objects to demonstrate this continuity, this book examined the visual fields of racial violence during the eras of Reconstruction and the post-Mexican-American War period of manifest destiny. This framing shows how violence performed a function parallel and similar to that of the televised displays of police violence in the contemporary post-1965 period of late capital crisis, policing, and superincarceration. By first presenting a provisional map of the relationship between these two seemingly disparate textual objects, the chapters reveal the ideological work of the institutional structures that mobilize our vision and the practice of witnessing. This centrality of vision, the ocularcentrism of modern society, grants a privileged place to seeing and looking in the construction of knowledge. As a result, to *know* the world occurs through regimes of a visuality that strengthens the power of truth and empiricism as they are central to the projects of colonialism, militarism, and White supremacy. Institutions—particularly those that rely on the Enlightenment projects of science and technology for their legitimacy—function as stations of power that simultaneously force and create our seeing and order the world in often violent ways.

To untether history from empiricism, we can consider Benjamin's plea to recognize moments of danger as they flash before us as a call to action against the interested function of historical narrative. Holding a theoretical mirror to history, the reflection of spectacular racial violence in relation to crisis and accumulation is a material genealogy of legal and extralegal violence. This book is an attempt to reconcile the past with its refracted present and to examine the continued way in which we as a public *live with* practices of racial punishment and violence. The conditions of possibility for racial discipline—the moments when material value could be constituted through the disciplining of the racial body—can be seen in the visuals of past racial violence and the documentation of bodies across the United States. The criminalization of African Americans, Native Americans, Mexicans, and Asians and the visible destruction of the racial body serve to further the projects of national becoming in an unapologetic narrative of domination shared by the collective public sphere and the representational tools (material and ideological) marshaled to render spectacular violence everyday, mundane, and acceptable. The refractions of history's mirror were exhibited via the similarities between the two periods—that is, between the era of Reconstruction and the settling of the Southwest and the post-1965, post-Fordist period of deindustrialization and globalization.

These moments of danger are marked by the lynched bodies, which displayed through their dismemberment the anxieties of the crisis-ridden Reconstruction and post-Reconstruction era, that reappeared almost 150 years later in the museum exhibition and photo art book *Without Sanctuary*. This provided their late twentieth-century audience a moment of opportunity to recognize the past in the present. The rewitnessing of racial punishment was a missed opportunity. The resurrection of this past and the respectacularization of those bodies served only to reveal the veiled agreements between the past and the present. In their shock, twenty-first-century spectators could only reconcile themselves to the images they viewed through the discourse of the lessons of history and healing, a vacant script of humanitarian progress unattached to the material value of the disciplined body.

The sole continuity that viewers and commentators traced relied on an excessively literal (mis)understanding of lynching. The names of Abner Louima, Amadou Diallo, and James Byrd, and later the prisoners of Abu Ghraib, were invoked as evidence that the country had not evolved from its brutal past, and, although the level of brutality against Louima, Diallo, Byrd, and the prisoners of Abu Ghraib indicates that the United States has not broken with the history of racial terror, it has shifted under the liberal ideals of progress and reconciliation. However, it is clear that those private and concealed instances of racial violence do not represent a contemporary analogue to lynching, which was necessarily a public act, an act whose efficacy depended on its being *viewed*. The fact of this critique left the public blind to its complicity with the true heir to that era of violent racial spectacle—the repressive work of the state performed publicly night after night on the television show *COPS*.

And it is in *COPS* where the longer trajectory of the visual regimes of racial discipline discussed in the previous chapters can be seen more clearly. The "reality" depicted on and created by *COPS* signified and provided evidence for social truths used to justify the violent policing of people of color and the poor under the guise of progress and professionalism. The spectacle shifted both from a practice of the absolute and unapologetic destruction of the body at the hands of an "unofficial" policing group—the lynching mobs—to the more blandly technocratic forms of discipline and destruction performed by the modern police state and from a homogeneous racial practice of White-on-Black violence to one that is heterogeneous and complex, revealing that the violence serves the inherent interest of the accumulation of White Humanity.

I attempt in this work to break through the blinders of the everyday, to push through the ideological bonds of that most confining straitjacket—the world as it is seen. What we see as amusing and what we see as unspeakably barbarous can turn out to be the same. What does this say about us? Perhaps that we know ourselves poorly, that our memories are short, and that amnesia can be worse than fatal. "What one does not remember," James Baldwin wrote, "is the serpent in the garden of one's dreams." It is more than that though. The reasons we critique are to place the blame properly, to ferret out lies, and also to chase a world as yet unseen. Baldwin goes on: "What one does not remember contains the only hope."[1]

Notes

INTRODUCTION

1. Ofelia Cuevas, *Race and the LA Human: Race Relations and Violence in Globalized Los Angeles*, in *Black and Brown in Los Angeles: Beyond Conflict and Coalition*, ed. Josh Kun and Laura Pulido (Berkeley: University of California Press, 2014). Jordan Camp and Cristina Heatherton, *Policing the Planet: Why the Policing Crisis Led to Black Lives Matter* (New York: Verso, 2016). Kelly Lytle-Hernandez, *City of Inmates: Conquest, Rebellion and the Rise of Human Caging in Los Angeles 1771–1965* (Chapel Hill: University of North Carolina Press, 2016).

2. Elizabeth Alexander, "The Trayvon Generation," *New Yorker*, June 15, 2020.

3. Ruth Gilmore, *Golden Gulag: Prisons, Surplus, Crisis, and Opposition in Globalizing California* (Berkeley: University of California Press, 2006).

4. Richard Zoglin, "The Networks Run for Cover," *Time*, December 14, 1990, 83.

5. Walter Benjamin, "Theses on the Philosophy of History," in *Illuminations*, ed. Hannah Arendt (New York: Random House, 1968).

6. Benjamin, "Theses on the Philosophy of History," 255.

CHAPTER 1

1. See the discussion of the prison's relationship to popular culture and genre in Angela Y. Davis's *Are Prisons Obsolete?* (New York: Seven Stories, 2003), 17. Davis cites Gina Dent stating that the history of film has always been wedded to the representation of incarceration dating back to 1901 and Thomas Edison's first films, including *The Execution of Czolgosz, with Panorama of Auburn Prison*.

2. A. Davis, *Are Prisons Obsolete?* 18.

3. A. Davis, 18.

4. Hal Foster, *Vision and Visuality* (Seattle: Bay, 1988), ix.

5. Irit Rogoff, ed., *The Visual Culture Reader* (London: Routledge, 1998), 25.

6. Rogoff, *The Visual Culture Reader*, 25.

7. Martin Jay, *Downcast Eyes: The Denigration of Vision in Twentieth-Century French Thought* (Berkeley: University of California Press, 1993).

8. See Foster, *Vision and Visuality*.

9. Donna Haraway, *Simians, Cyborgs, and Women: The Reinvention of Nature* (London: Free Association Books, 1991), 188.

10. See Haraway, *Simians, Cyborgs, and Women* 188.

11. See Haraway, *Simians, Cyborgs, and Women*, 189.

12. Michael Taussig, *Shamanism, Colonialism and the Wild Man: A Study in Terror and Healing* (Chicago: University of Chicago Press, 1987), xiii. Taussig names as *fictions of the real* and *epistemic murk* the making of social reality/ies in the highlands of Colombia during the rubber trade and horrible brutalities against the Putumayo Indians. Taussig explains how the official reports from the field, the ethnodocumentation of the Putumayo sent back to England, were the necessary representations of the lives and culture of the Native people that justified murder and violence against them. If terror thrives on the production of epistemic murk and metamorphosis, it nevertheless requires the hermeneutic violence of epistemic murk and fictions of the real as mechanisms of power that both justify and entertain.

13. Judith Butler, "Endangered/Endangering: Schematic Racism and White Paranoia," in *Reading Rodney King/Reading Urban Uprising*, ed. Robert Gooding-Williams (New York: Routledge, 1993), 16.

14. Butler, "Endangered/Endangering," 15.

15. Benjamin, "Theses on the Philosophy of History."

16. Yvonne Jewkes, *Media and Crime* (London: Sage, 2004), 4.

17. Christopher P. Campbell, *Race, Myth and the News* (Thousand Oaks, CA: Sage, 1995), 28.

18. Franklin D. Gilliam Jr. and Shanto Iyengar, "Prime Suspects: The Influence of Local Television News on the Viewing Public," *American Journal of Political Science* 44, no. 3 (2000): 560–573.

19. George Gerbner and Larry Gross, "Living with Television: The Violence Profile," *Journal of Communication* 25, no. 2 (1976): 173–199; Joseph Dominick, "Crime and Law Enforcement on Prime-Time Television," *Public Opinion Quarterly* 37, no. 2 (1973): 241–250; Doris Graber, *Crime News and the Public* (New York: Praeger, 1980).

20. Annette Hill, *Reality TV: Audiences and Popular Factual Television* (London: Routledge, 2005); Su Holmes and Deborah Jermyn, *Understanding Reality Television* (London: Routledge, 2004).

21. Mark Fishman and Gray Cavendar, eds. *Entertaining Crime: Television Reality Programs* (New York: Aldine De Gruyter, 1998), 5.

22. Fishman and Cavendar, *Entertaining Crime*, 13.

23. Mary Beth Oliver and G. Blake Armstrong, "The Color of Crime: Perceptions of Caucasians' and African Americans' Involvement in Crime," in *Entertaining Crime: Television Reality Programs*, ed. Mark Fishman and Gray Cavendar (New York: Aldine De Gruyter, 1998).

24. James Carlson, *Primetime Law Enforcement: Crime Show Viewing and Attitudes toward the Criminal Justice System* (New York: Praeger, 1985); Garrett O'Keefe, *Public Views on Crime: Television Exposure and Media Credibility* (Thousand Oaks: Sage, 1984).

25. Kathryn K. Russell, *The Color of Crime: Racial Hoaxes, White Fear, Black Protectionism, Police Harassment and Other Macroaggressions* (New York: New York University Press, 1998), xiii, 3.

26. Russell, *Color of Crime*, 17.

27. Russell, 19. The Slave Codes denied enslaved people political, social, and economic equalities. They were denied the right to vote, own property, and marry and were judged by separate tribunals that included different procedural practices. Although the Black Codes, instituted in 1865, entitled Black people to marry and enter into legal contracts, they also included laws that restricted mobility, agency, and property, such as codes against vagrancy, unemployment, employment licensing (the right to become a storekeeper, mechanic, or artisan), assembly, and the ownership of arms. Jim Crow segregation statutes instituted segregationist practices that regulated public space (i.e., access to hospitals, cemeteries, public restrooms, trains, and churches) and behavior (i.e., properly addressing white people, interracial relationships, and racial etiquette).

28. Alex Lichtenstein, *Twice the Work of Free Labor: The Political Economy of Convict Labor in the New South* (New York: Verso, 1996); Luanna Ross, *Inventing the Savage: The Social Construction of Native American Criminality* (Austin: University of Texas Press, 1998); Americo Paredes, *"With a Pistol in His Hand": A Border Ballad and Its Hero* (Austin: University of Texas Press, 1958).

29. See Russell, *Color of Crime*, 25, where Russell lists what she believes are the minimal requirements for a fair criminal justice system: "1. Criminal penalties that apply to everyone regardless of the race of the offender. 2. Criminal penalties that apply to everyone equally regardless of the race of the victim. 3. The race of the offender is not relevant in determining whether his actions constitute a crime. The offender's actions would have been considered criminal, even if he were another race. 4. The race of the victim is not relevant in determining whether the offenders action constitutes a crime. 5. The offender's racial pedigree is not used to determine punishment. 6. There are checks and balances that mitigate against racial bias within the legal system."

30. See Gilmore's analysis in *Golden Gulag*.

31. Ariella Azoulay, *The Civil Contract of Photography* (Brooklyn: Zone Books, 2012).

32. Courtney Baker, *Humane Insight: Looking at Images of African American Suffering and Death* (Urbana: University of Illinois Press, 2015), x.

33. Avery Gordon, *Ghostly Matters: Haunting and the Sociological Imagination* (Minneapolis: University of Minnesota Press, 1997), 5.

34. Gordon, *Ghostly Matters*, 20.

35. Gordon, 21.

36. Gordon, 7.

37. See Foster, *Vision and Visuality*.

38. Ofelia Ortiz Cuevas, "Arresting Images: *COPS* in the 'Projects' of Race" (master's thesis, University of California, San Diego, 2000).

39. "Bennett under Fire for Remarks . . . ," CNN, September 30, 2005, available at https://www.cnn.com/2005/POLITICS/09/30/bennett.comments/index.html.

40. Jean Baudrillard, *Simulacra and Simulation* (Ann Arbor: University of Michigan Press, 1994).

41. On this point, see Jay, *Downcast Eyes*; Deborah Poole, *Vision, Race and Modernity: A Visual Economy of the Andean Image* (Princeton, NJ: Princeton University Press, 1997); Fatimah Tobing Rony, *The Third Eye: Race, Cinema and the Ethnographic Spectacle* (Durham, NC: Duke University Press, 1996); John Tagg, *The Burden of Representation: Essays on Photographies and Histories* (Minneapolis: University of Minnesota Press, 1993).

42. Barbara Marie Stafford, *Body Criticism: Imaging the Unseen in Enlightenment Art and Medicine* (Cambridge, MA: MIT Press, 1993); Chrissy Illes and Russell Roberts, *Visible*

Light: Photography and Classification in Art, Science and the Everyday (Oxford: Museum of Modern Art, 1997).

43. Shawn Michelle Smith, *American Archives: Gender, Race, and Class in Visual Culture* (Princeton, NJ: Princeton University Press, 1999), 125. See also Joshua Cole, *The Power of Large Numbers: Population, Politics and Gender in 19th Century France* (Ithaca, NY: Cornell University Press, 2000), 112. Using this method, along with other techniques that differentiate people based on physical characteristics and race, resembles the written realism of the documentation of "native" life taken by European governing bodies. Early European racial theory could be read by only small groups of people. Photography was the first means by which this information was circulated to the public.

44. Robert Cooter, *Cultural Meaning of Popular Science: Phrenology and the Organization of Consent in Nineteenth Century Britain* (Cambridge: Cambridge University Press, 1984), 79. Cooter explains that "Gall's physiological psychology, by uniting the mind with the neurology on one hand and the biology of adaptation on the other, seemed a conceptual triumph of the highest order, for it transformed abstract metaphysical conceptions of mind into actual organic entities amenable to the interest and understandings of the practical mind" (32).

45. See Rony, *Third Eye*; Anne McClintock, *Imperial Leather: Race, Gender, and Sexuality in the Colonial Contest* (New York: Routledge, 1995); Lisa Cartwright, *Screening the Body: Tracing Medicine's Visual Culture* (Minneapolis: University of Minnesota Press, 1998).

46. Donna Haraway, "Teddy Bear Patriarchy: Taxidermy in the Garden of Eden, New York City 1908–1936," in *Culture/Power/History: A Reader in Contemporary Theory*, ed. Nicholas B. Dirks, Geoff Eley, and Sherry B. Ortner (Princeton, NJ: Princeton University Press, 1994), 51.

47. Laura Mulvey, *Visual and Other Pleasures* (Indianapolis: Indiana University Press, 1989).

48. John Fabian, *Time and the Other* (New York: Columbia University Press, 1983).

49. Fabian, *Time and the Other*, 5.

50. Tony Bennett, "The Exhibitionary Complex," in *Culture/Power/History: A Reader in Contemporary Theory*, ed. Nicholas B. Dirks, Geoff Eley, and Sherry B. Ortner (Princeton, NJ: Princeton University Press, 1994).

51. According to Peter Linebaugh in *The London Hanged: Crime and Civil Society in the Eighteenth Century* (Cambridge: Cambridge University Press, 1992), in the early modern period emperors and kings cultivated spectacles as part of their rituals of governance. Machiavelli advised his modern prince of the productive use of governance and social control. Later, in preindustrial London, the bodies hung from the gallows of Tyburn embodied the modern conceptions of time, labor control, and capital.

52. Michel Foucault, *Discipline and Punish* (New York: Vintage, 1975).

53. See Joy James's critique of Foucault's inability to account for the persistence of racial violence in "Erasing the Spectacle of Racialized State Violence," in *Resisting State Violence: Radicalism, Gender and Race in US Culture* (Minneapolis: University of Minnesota Press, 1996).

54. Ken Gonzalez-Day, *Lynching in the West, 1850–1935* (Durham, NC: Duke University Press, 2006), 11.

55. Guy Debord, *The Society of the Spectacle* (Detroit: Black and Red, 1977), 43.

56. In this book, I do not use the word "spectacle" in the same sense as Debord—as the overarching mediation of social relationships by commodified images. I use the term more narrowly to refer to specific sites of mediation because it is important to consider

spectacle as a (visual) vehicle for the construction of the racial body. Of course, the realm of the spectacle has changed—spectacle does not take place beneath the hangman's scaffold but on television and the internet. Spectacle on *COPS* becomes commodified and brings the spectacle of violence back to the gathering crowds, now in the privacy of the home.

57. Allen Feldman, *Formations of Violence: The Narrative of the Body and Political Terror in Northern Ireland* (Chicago: University of Chicago Press, 1991).

58. Peter Stallybrass and Allon White, *The Politics and Poetics of Transgression* (Ithaca, NY: Cornell University Press, 1986), 42.

59. See Mikhail Bakhtin's *The Dialogic Imagination: Four Essays* (Austin: University of Texas Press, 1981) and Bakhtin's *Rabelais and His World* (Cambridge, MA: MIT Press, 1968).

60. Stallybrass and White, *Politics and Poetics of Transgression*, 23.

61. Stallybrass and White, 22.

62. Hannah Arendt, *Eichmann in Jerusalem: A Report on the Banality of Evil* (New York: Viking, 1964), 156.

63. Raymond Williams, *Marxism and Literature* (Oxford: Oxford University Press, 1977), 132.

64. Williams, *Marxism and Literature*, 132.

CHAPTER 2

1. See Gilmore, *Golden Gulag*; A. Davis, *Are Prisons Obsolete?* Tara Herivel and Paul Wright, *Prison Nation: The Warehousing of America's Poor* (New York: Routledge, 2002); Marc Mauer, *Race to Incarcerate* (New York: New Press, 2006).

2. Center on Juvenile and Criminal Justice, "Executive Summary: America's One-Million Nonviolent Offenders," March 1999, available at http://www.cjcj.org/uploads/cjcj /documents/americas.pdf.

3. United Nations Human Rights Committee, "In the Shadows of the War on Terror: Persistent Police Brutality and Abuse in the United States," May 2006.

4. In 2000, the U.S. Commission on Civil Rights and the National Institute of Justice submitted a report to Congress stating that the wrongful use of force by police is indiscernible due to a lack of comprehensive national data. See Geoffrey P. Albert and Roger G. Dunham, "Analysis of Police Use of Force Data," July 25, 2000, available at http://www .ncjrs.gov/pdffiles1/nij/grants/183648.pdf.

5. A. Davis, *Are Prisons Obsolete?* 25.

6. W.E.B. Du Bois, *Black Reconstruction in America* (New York: Atheneum, 1935), 125.

7. Matthew J. Mancini, "Race, Economics, and the Abandonment of Convict Lease," *Journal of Negro History* 63, no. 4 (1978): 339–352.

8. Ida B. Wells, *On Lynching, Southern Horrors, A Red Record, Mob Rule in New Orleans* (New York: Arno, 1969).

9. Wells, *On Lynching*, 16.

10. Wells, 16.

11. Benjamin, "Theses on the Philosophy of History," 254.

12. Benjamin, 254.

13. Walter Burns, *The Robin Hood of El Dorado: The Saga of Joaquin Murrieta, Famous Outlaw of California's Age of Gold* (Albuquerque: University of New Mexico Press, 1999).

14. Richard E. Jensen, R. Eli Paul, and John E. Carter, *Eyewitness at Wounded Knee* (Lincoln: University of Nebraska Press, 2011).

15. Jensen, Paul, and Carter, *Eyewitness at Wounded Knee*, x.

16. Jensen, Paul, and Carter.

17. I put these words in italics to highlight the negligible differences between the two and the problematic way in which the insistence on this differentiation by both scholars who study the criminal justice system and those who study the history of violence continues to occlude the systemic institutionalization of rational brutality.

18. James Baldwin, *The Evidence of Things Not Seen* (New York: Henry Holt, 1985), 42.

19. See Edward L. Ayers, *Vengeance and Justice: Crime and Punishment in the Nineteenth Century American South* (New York: Oxford University Press, 1984); Richard Brown, *Strain of Violence: Historical Studies of American Violence and Vigilantism* (New York: Oxford University Press, 1975); Lawrence Friedman, *Crime and Punishment in American History* (New York: Basic Books, 1993); Christopher Waldrep, *The Many Faces of Judge Lynch* (New York: Palgrave, 2002).

20. Lauren Berlant, *The Queen of America Goes to Washington: Essays on Sex and Citizenship* (Durham, NC: Duke University Press, 1997), 4.

21. See Ayers, *Vengeance and Justice*; Friedman, *Crime and Punishment in American History*.

22. Steven Bright, "Discrimination, Death, and Denial: Race and the Death Penalty," in *Machinery of Death: The Reality of America's Death Penalty Regime*, ed. David Dow and Mark Dow (New York: Routledge, 2002). Two of the largest acts of discipline held for public viewing were against racial minorities. In December 1865, a military tribunal sentenced 303 Dakota people to death for charges of murder and rape in the Dakota War of 1862. Sanctioned by President Lincoln, 38 Dakota people were hung in front of a crowd of an estimated 3,000 men, women, and children, in Mankato, Minnesota. The second largest was the public hanging of 13 Black soldiers for their part in the Houston Riot of 1917.

23. Cheryl Harris, "Whiteness as Property," *Harvard Law Review* 106, no. 8 (1993): 1714.

24. Harris, "Whiteness as Property," 1720.

25. Harris, 1720.

26. Harris, 1721.

27. John A. Carpenter, "Atrocities in the Reconstruction Period," *Journal of Negro History* 47, no. 4 (1962): 234–247; Christopher Waldrep and Donald Nieman, *Local Matters: Race, Crime and Justice in the Nineteenth Century South* (Athens: University of Georgia Press, 2001), 22.

28. Bentham cited in Harris, "Whiteness as Property," 1729.

29. Harris, "Whiteness," 1730.

30. W. R. Brock, *An American Crisis: Congress and Reconstruction, 1865–1867* (London: Macmillan, 1963), 25. See, also, Eric Foner, "Reconstruction Revisited," *Reviews in American History*, 10, no. 4 (1982): 82–100.

31. Horace Mann Bond, "Social and Economic Forces in Alabama Reconstruction," *Journal of Negro History* 23, no 3 (1938): 290–348.

32. Du Bois, *Black Reconstruction*, 167.

33. See P. A. Taylor, *Professor Huxley on the Negro Question*, Ladies' London Emancipation Society, 1864, available at https://mathcs.clarku.edu/huxley/comm/Books/Taylor.html.

34. A. Everette James, "Images of African Americans in Southern Paintings 1840–1940," *Southern Cultures* 9, no. 2 (2003): 67–81.

35. Horace Mann Bond, "Social and Economic Forces in Alabama Reconstruction."

36. Sandra Gunning, *Race, Rape, and Lynching: The Red Record of American Literature* (New York: Oxford University Press, 1996), 21.

37. Gunning, *Race, Rape, and Lynching*, 22.

38. Mario Barrera, *Race and Class in the Southwest: A Theory of Racial Inequality* (Notre Dame, IN: University of Notre Dame Press, 1980); Neil Foley, *White Scourge: Mexicans, Blacks and Poor Whites in Texas Cotton Culture* (Berkeley: University of California Press, 1997).

39. Reginald Horseman, *Race and Manifest Destiny: Origins of American Racial Anglo Saxonism* (Cambridge, MA: Harvard University Press, 1981), 105.

40. Reginald Horseman, *Race and Manifest Destiny*.

41. David J. Weber, *Myth and the History of the Hispanic Southwest* (Albuquerque: University of New Mexico Press, 1987), 157.

42. Paredes, *With a Pistol in His Hand*, 16.

43. See Rudolfo Acuna, *Occupied America: A History of Chicanos* (New York: Harper and Row, 1988); David Montejano, *Anglos and Mexicans in the Making of Texas, 1836–1986* (Austin: University of Texas Press, 1987).

44. Paredes, *With a Pistol in His Hand*, 35.

45. William D. Carrigan and Clive Webb, "The Lynching of Persons of Mexican Origin or Descent in the US, 1848 to 1928," *Journal of Social History* 37, no. 2 (2003): 411–438.

46. Robert Berkhoter, *The White Man's Indian: Images of the American Indian from Columbus to the Present* (New York: Random House, 1979).

47. Ross, *Inventing the Savage*, 57.

48. Ross, 35.

49. Wolfgang Mieder, "'The Only Good Indian Is a Dead One': History and Meaning of a Proverbial Stereotype," *Journal of American Folklore* 106, no. 419 (1993): 38–60.

50. Mieder, "The Only Good Indian Is a Dead One."

51. Charles McClain, *In Search of Equality: The Chinese Struggle against Discrimination in the Nineteenth Century* (Berkeley: University of California Press, 1996).

52. Jimmie Reeves and Richard Campbell, *Cracked Coverage: Television News, the Anti-Cocaine Crusade, and the Reagan Legacy* (Durham, NC: Duke University Press, 1994); Herman Gray, *Watching Race: Television and the Struggle for "Blackness"* (Minneapolis: University of Minnesota Press, 1995), 43.

53. On the history of the criminalization and the vilification of Chinese immigrants and Chinese Americans in San Francisco, see Nayan Shah, *Contagious Divides: Epidemics and Race in San Francisco's Chinatown* (Berkeley: University of California Press, 2001).

54. Barry Bluestone and Bennett Harrison, *The Deindustrialization of America: Plant Closings, Community Abandonment, and the Dismantling of Basic Industry* (New York: Basic Books, 1982), 9.

55. Bluestone and Harrison, *Deindustrialization of America*, 10.

56. Bluestone and Harrison, 15. For example, during the 1970s, GE expanded its worldwide payroll by five thousand employees because of the hiring of an additional thirty thousand nonunion low-wage foreign workers. RCA cut U.S. employment by fourteen thousand workers while it increased its nonunionized foreign workforce by nineteen thousand. At the same time, Ford Motor Company spent 40 percent of its budget outside the United States and General Motors built one of its largest plants initially planned for Kansas City in Spain. Bluestone and Harrison state that somewhere between thirty-two million and thirty-eight million jobs were lost during the 1970s.

57. Morris Morely and James Petras, "Wealth and Poverty in the National Economy: The Domestic Foundations of Clinton's Global Policy," in *Social Policy and the Conservative Agenda*, ed. Clarence Y. H. Lo and Michael Schwartz (New York: Blackwell, 1998), 122.

58. Saskia Sassen, *Globalization and Its Discontents: Essays in the New Mobility of People and Money* (New York: New Press, 142).

59. Sassen, *Globalization and Its Discontents*. Rene Tagima-Peña and Christine Choy provide an excellent example of the effects of the idea of the "villainous Japanese" in their documentary, *Who Killed Vincent Chin?* an account of the murder of Vincent Chin, a Chinese American killed by two white displaced auto workers in Detroit.

60. George Gilder, *Wealth and Poverty* (New York: Bantam Books, 1982).

61. Bluestone and Harrison, *Deindustrialization of America*, 5.

62. Bluestone and Harrison, 35.

63. Angela Y. Davis, "Race and Criminalization: Black Americans and the Punishment Industry," in *The House That Race Built*, ed. Wahneema Lubiano (New York: Pantheon, 1997).

64. John Fiske, *Media Matters: Everyday Culture and Political Change* (Minneapolis: University of Minnesota Press, 1994), 93. See also the original ad, available at https://www.youtube.com/watch?v=Io9KMSSEZ0Y.

65. Michael Rogin, *Ronald Reagan, the Movie: And Other Episodes in Political Demonology* (Berkeley: University of California Press, 1987), xvii.

66. Mike Davis, *City of Quartz* (New York: Verso, 1990), 272.

67. M. Davis, *City of Quartz*, 281.

68. Louis Sahagun, "Former First Lady, Gates on Scene as SWAT Team Carries Out Drug Raid," *Los Angeles Times*, April 8, 1989.

69. M. Davis, *City of Quartz*, 225.

70. See these books by Eugene Genovese, *Roll Jordon Roll: The World the Slaves Made* (New York: Vintage, 1976) and *From Rebellion to Revolution: Afro-American Slave Revolts in the Making of the Modern World* (Baton Rouge: Louisiana State University Press, 1992).

71. A. Davis, *Are Prisons Obsolete?* 45.

72. Du Bois, *Black Reconstruction*, 167.

73. Du Bois, 178. Du Bois explains that the policing and patrolling of Black people began in the antebellum South and were made possible by a special police force composed of a large number of poor white people in the South. Poor white people could be employed as overseers, slave drivers, or other members of the patrolling system. This system continued into the Reconstruction era.

74. Louisiana Black Codes, "The Black Code of St. Landry's Parish, Louisiana," 1865.

75. Du Bois, *Black Reconstruction*, 12.

76. Mary Ellen Curtin, *Black Prisoners and Their World, Alabama 1865–1900* (Charlottesville: University of Virginia Press, 2000), 34.

77. Curtin, *Black Prisoners and Their World*, 43.

78. David Oshinsky, *Worse Than Slavery: Parchman Farm and the Ordeal of Jim Crow Justice* (New York: Free Press, 1996).

79. Lichtenstein, *Twice the Work of Free Labor*, 106. Lichtenstein states that the building of Georgia's modern transportation structures relied on Black convict labor.

80. Matthew J. Mancini, *One Dies, Get Another: Convict Leasing in the American South, 1866–1928* (Columbia: University of South Carolina Press, 1996), 151.

81. Mancini, *One Dies, Get Another*, 151.

82. Oshinsky, *Worse Than Slavery*, 87.

83. A. Davis, *Are Prisons Obsolete?* 31.

84. Oshinsky, *Worse Than Slavery*, 43.

85. Christian Parenti, *Lockdown America: Police and Prisons in the Age of Crisis* (New York: Verso, 1999).

86. Parenti, *Lockdown America*, 6.

87. During this time period, there was a shift from a civil rights struggle for voting and housing to resistance to state power such as the Black Power movement, which included struggles over police brutality and the development of community-run food programs, the Brown Power movement, which included struggles over land rights and the Treaty of Guadalupe Hidalgo through the activism of people like Reies Lopez Tijerina, and the American Indian movement at Wounded Knee.

88. Parenti, *Lockdown America*, 112. After the Watts riots, a report by then governor Pat Brown attributed the outbreak to a social and economic situation that needed to be addressed by state programs. As a young LAPD officer, Daryl Gates's response to Watts was to develop a militarized strategy that resulted in instituting SWAT teams and was heavily funded with both state and federal funding. SWAT's first job was a raid on the Black Panther offices in downtown Los Angeles.

89. Interestingly, the first action supported by the LEAA was at a small historically black college in 1970 (Mississippi Valley State University), where students had initiated a strike to change conditions. The strike was 95 percent effective. The LEAA was brought in to break the strike and over twenty-five hundred students, almost one-third of the student body, were arrested.

90. According to Parenti's *Lockdown America*, a report on CBS showed U.S. soldiers smoking marijuana through the barrel of a rifle and one soldier testified to Congress that at least 60 percent of the unit involved in the My Lai incident had smoked marijuana at least once.

91. Parenti, *Lockdown America*, 25.

92. Jerome Miller, *Search and Destroy: African American Males in the Criminal Justice System* (Cambridge: Cambridge University Press, 1996), 3.

93. U.S. Department of Justice, "State and Federal Prison Population, 1960–1994," Bureau of Justice Statistics, Washington, DC.

94. Human Rights Watch, *Incarcerated America: Human Rights Watch Backgrounder*, April 2003, available at https://www.hrw.org/legacy/backgrounder/usa/incarceration /us042903.pdf. See also the Sentencing Project's "State Rates of Incarceration by Race," May 2004.

CHAPTER 3

1. Mary Thomas, "'Without Sanctuary' Digs Deeply into Painful Issues of Inhumanity," *Post-Gazette Art Review*, September 29, 2001.

2. James Allen, ed., *Without Sanctuary: Lynching Photography in America* (Santa Fe, NM: Twin Palms, 2000).

3. John Lewis, "Foreword," in *Without Sanctuary: Lynching Photography in America* (Santa Fe, NM: Twin Palms, 2000), 7.

4. Marita Sturken, *Tangled Memories: The Vietnam War, the AIDS Epidemic and the Politics of Remembering* (Berkeley: University of California Press, 1997), 8.

5. A "picker" is someone who searches the countryside for art, treasure, discards, or things that people do not want in order to sell them to someone who does.

6. Mike Downey, "An American Holocaust," *Los Angeles Times Home Edition*, February 6, 2000.

7. Melanie Peeples, "'Without Sanctuary': Artifacts of Lynching in America," *Tavis Smiley Show*, National Public Radio, May 6, 2004, available at http://www.npr.org/templates /story/story.php?storyId=1874649.

8. Op-Ed Editor, "America's Unfinished Business," *Copley News Service*, May 14, 2002.

9. Thomas, "'Without Sanctuary' Digs Deeply into Inhumanity."

10. Brent Staples, "The Perils of Growing Comfortable with Evil," *New York Times*, April 9, 2000.

11. Staples, "Perils of Growing Comfortable with Evil." Staples's reference to Sontag was recurring and refers to her works *On Photography* and *Regarding the Pain of Others*.

12. Cynthia Carr, "The Atrocity Exhibition," *Village Voice*, March 28, 2000.

13. Sarah Valdez, "American Abject; Exhibition; Without Sanctuary: Lynching Photography in America," *Art in America*, October 1, 2000.

14. Valdez, "American Abject."

15. Cary Clack, "A Vow: Never Again—Images of Hate Must Compel Nation to Confront Racism," *San Antonio Express-News*, February 6, 2000.

16. J. Allen, *Without Sanctuary*, 204.

17. Kathy Janich, "Line Steady for Last View of Lynching Photographs," *Atlanta Journal-Constitution*, January 13, 2003.

18. J. Allen, *Without Sanctuary*, 9.

19. J. Allen, 21.

20. J. Allen, 21.

21. J. Allen, 21.

22. J. R. Moehringer, "Scavenger or Voyeur? Why Did James Allen Collect Pictures of Lynchings in America and Ask Us to Look at Them?" *Calgary Herald*, October 21, 2000.

23. Moehringer, "Scavenger or Voyeur?"

24. J. Allen, *Without Sanctuary*.

25. Paige Parvin, "Strange Fruit: Emory Takes a Hard Look at One of America's Deepest Sorrows," *Emory Magazine* (Summer 2002).

26. Parvin, "Strange Fruit."

27. Op-Ed Editor, "America's Unfinished Business."

28. George Fredrickson, "For African Americans, Justice Was Often at the End of a Rope: Lynching Photography in America," *Journal of Blacks in Higher Education* 28 (Summer 2000): 126.

29. Duane J. Corpis and Ian Christopher Fletcher, "Without Sanctuary," *Radical History Review* (Winter 2003): 284.

30. It is important to consider the use of this term in contemporary debates over the persecution of Black males. Shawn Michelle Smith notes that "modern-day lynching" has been used discursively in the cases of Clarence Thomas, Mike Tyson, and O. J. Simpson. In addition, there were numerous references to what I call memorable tragedies; the list includes the killing of Matthew Shepard, the bombing of women's health clinics, and 9/11.

31. Susan Sontag, "Regarding the Torture of Others," *New York Times*, May 23, 2004.

32. Sontag, "Regarding the Torture of Others."

33. Sontag.

34. Hazel Carby, "A Strange and Bitter Crop: The Spectacle of Torture," *Open Democracy*, October 10, 2004, available at https://www.opendemocracy.net/en/article_2149jsp/.

CHAPTER 4

1. Cuevas, "Arresting Images," 2.

2. Denise da Silva, *Toward a Global Idea of Race* (Minneapolis: University of Minnesota Press, 2007).

3. da Silva, *Toward a Global Idea of Race*.

4. James Wolcott, "Car 54, Where Are You?" *New Yorker*, February 8, 1993.

5. Charles Lane, "Editorial," *New Republic*, April 3, 1995.

6. Rony, *Third Eye*.

7. Robin Kelley, *Yo' Mama's Disfunktional: Fighting the Culture Wars in Urban America*. (Boston: Beacon, 1997), 18.

8. Kelley, *Yo' Mama's Disfunktional*, 20.

9. Cuevas, "Arresting Images."

10. Fishman and Cavendar, *Entertaining Crime*.

11. See Reeves and Campbell, *Cracked Coverage*; Gray, *Watching Race*; John Fiske, *Media Matters* (Minneapolis: University of Minnesota Press, 1996).

12. Gray, *Watching Race*, 17.

13. Gray, 17.

14. Gray, 17.

15. Sut Jhally and Justin Lewis, *Enlightened Racism: The Bill Cosby Show, Audiences, and the Myth of the American Dream* (Boulder, CO: Westview, 1992).

16. Gray, *Watching Race*, 68.

17. George Lipsitz, "The Possessive Investment in Whiteness: Racialized Social Democracy and the 'White' Problem in American Studies," *American Quarterly* 47, no. 3 (September 1995): 369.

18. Cuevas, "Arresting Images." This is of critical importance considering the historical backdrop in which *COPS* takes place, as the 1980s symbolized wealth and economic prosperity, and poverty became criminal and deviant.

19. Stuart Hall, Chas Critcher, Tony Jefferson, John Clarke, and Brian Roberts, *Policing the Crisis: Mugging, the State and Law and Order* (London: Macmillan, 1978), 394.

20. I would maintain here that this argument is not to say that poor white people are equal to Black people, as white people experience the police state much differently than Black people do precisely because their relation to the state and capital is uniquely White.

21. Eric Lott, *Love and Theft: Black Face Minstrelsy and the American Working Class* (New York: Oxford University Press, 1993). Lott asserts that minstrelsy enabled the formation of a white working class, a white subject, in a dialectic opposition to Black socially and psychologically. Blackening up was a way in which the close proximity of the white working class to black people was distanced by black exaggeration but also the intimate psychological relations between high and low culture. Minstrel shows "capture an antebellum structure of racial feeling" that "brought to public form racialized elements of thought and feeling, tone and impulse, residing at the very edge of semantic availability, which Americans only dimly realized they felt, let alone understood." which came to represent the essence of Blackness in the popular imagination, 23.

22. Nicolaus Mills, *The Triumph of Meanness: America's War against Its Better Self* (Boston: Houghton Mifflin, 1997). The sentiment toward poverty over the past twenty years has changed. According to Mills, Ronald Reagan made the denial of compassion respectable, especially in regard to the poor, 2.

23. Stallybrass and White, *Politics and Poetics of Transgression*, 42.

24. Stallybrass and White, 22.

25. W.E.B. Du Bois, *Black Reconstruction in America 1860–1880* (New York: Simon and Schuster, 1935), 12.

26. Gilliam and Iyengar, "Prime Suspects."

27. Nicolas Blomley, "Law, Property and the Geography of Violence: The Frontier, the Survey and the Grid." *Annals of the Association of American Geographers* 93, no. 1 (2003): 122.

28. Blomley, "Law, Property and the Geography of Violence," 122.

29. John Baugh, *Beyond Ebonics Linguistic Pride and Racial Prejudice* (New York: Oxford University Press, 2000). During the Oakland Unified School District's attempt to establish Black English as distinct from English, in order to have Black English ESL programs instituted and funded by the state, Bill Clinton publicly termed it slang. Also, the U.S. secretary of education Richard Riley deemed it a nonstandard form of English and federal legislators prevented state and federal monies from funding any education program based on Black English.

30. Hall, *Policing the Crisis*, 341.

31. Earl Joseph, *Eloquence and Power: The Rise of Language Standards and Standard Languages* (London: Frances Pinter, 1987); James Milroy, *Authority in Language Prescription and Standardization* (London: Routledge, 1991). Regarding demands for linguistic standardization, there was a dramatic increase from the 1880s when linguistic faults where harshly criticized and an increase in the centralization and regulation of language occurred that can be seen in the development of the Oxford English Dictionary.

32. Erika Waddell, "John Langley: The Man Behind 'Cops,'" *Court TV*, available at http://www.courttv.com/onair/shows/hollywood_heat/articles/0505copsfeat1.html.

33. C. Riley Snorton, *Black on Both Sides: A Racial History of Trans Identity* (Minneapolis: University of Minnesota Press, 2017); Alexander Weheliye, *Habeas Viscus: Racialized Assemblages, Biopolitics, and Black Feminist Theories of the Human* (Durham, NC: Duke University Press, 2014).

34. bell hooks, *Talking Back: Thinking Feminist, Thinking Black* (Boston: South End, 1989).

35. George Lipsitz, *The Possessive Investment in Whiteness: How White People Profit from Identity Politics* (Philadelphia: Temple University Press, 1998), 116.

36. Robin Kelley, *Yo' Mama's Disfunktional: Fighting the Culture Wars in Urban America* (Boston: Beacon, 1997), 33.

37. Judith Stacey, "The Right Family Values," in *Social Policy and the Conservative Agenda*, ed. Clarence Y. H. Lo and Michael Schwartz (Malden, MA: Blackwell, 1998), 270.

38. Lipsitz, *Possessive Investment in Whiteness*, 116.

CONCLUSION

1. Baldwin, *Evidence of Things Not Seen*, xii.

Bibliography

Acuna, Rudolfo. *Occupied America: A History of Chicanos*. New York: Harper and Row, 1988.

Adamson, Christopher R. "Punishment after Slavery: Southern State Penal Systems, 1865–1890." *Social Problems* 30, no. 5 (1983): 555–569.

Albert, Geoffrey P., and Roger G. Dunham. "Analysis of Police Use of Force Data." July 25, 2000. Available at http://www.ncjrs.gov/pdffiles1/nij/grants/183648.pdf.

Allen, James, ed. *Without Sanctuary: Lynching Photography in America*. Santa Fe, NM: Twin Palms, 2000.

Allen, Robert. *Channels of Discourse*. Chapel Hill: University of North Carolina Press, 1987.

Almaguer, Tomas. *Racial Fault Lines: The Historical Origins of White Supremacy in California*. Berkeley: University of California Press, 1994.

Arendt, Hannah. *Eichmann in Jerusalem: A Report on the Banality of Evil*. New York: Viking, 1964.

Ayers, Edward L. *Vengeance and Justice: Crime and Punishment in the Nineteenth-Century American South*. New York: Oxford University Press, 1984.

Azoulay, Ariella. *The Civil Contract of Photography*. Brooklyn, NY: Zone Books, 2012.

Baker, Courtney. *Humane Insight: Looking at Images of African American Suffering and Death*. Urbana: University of Illinois Press, 2015.

Bakhtin, Mikhail. *The Dialogic Imagination: Four Essays*. Austin: University of Texas Press, 1981.

Baldwin, James. *The Evidence of Things Not Seen*. New York: Henry Holt & Co., 1985.

Balibar, Etienne, and Immanuel Wallerstein. *Race, Nation, Class: Ambiguous Identities*. New York: Verso, 1991.

Barrera, Mario. *Race and Class in the Southwest: A Theory of Racial Inequality*. Notre Dame, IN: University of Notre Dame Press, 1980.

Barthes, Roland. *Image Music Text*. New York: Hill and Wang, 1977.

Baudrillard, Jean. *Simulacra and Simulation.* Ann Arbor: University of Michigan Press, 1994.

Baugh, John. *Beyond Ebonics: Linguistic Pride and Racial Prejudice.* New York: Oxford University Press, 2000.

Benjamin, Walter. "Theses on the Philosophy of History." In *Illuminations*, edited by Hannah Arendt. New York: Random House, 1968.

Bennett, Tony. "The Exhibitionary Complex." In *Culture/Power/History: A Reader in Contemporary Theory*, edited by Nicholas B. Dirks, Geoff Eley, and Sherry B. Ortner. Princeton, NJ: Princeton University Press, 1994.

Berkhoter, Robert. *The White Man's Indian: Images of the American Indian from Columbus to the Present.* New York: Random House, 1979.

Berlant, Lauren. *The Queen of America Goes to Washington: Essays on Sex and Citizenship.* Durham, NC: Duke University Press, 1997.

Bernstein, Michael, and David Adler. *Understanding American Economic Decline.* Cambridge: Cambridge University Press, 1994.

Bluestone, Barry, and Bennett Harrison. *The Deindustrialization of America: Plant Closing, Community Abandonment, and the Dismantling of Basic Industry.* New York: Basic Books, 1982.

Bogle, Donald. *Toms, Coons, Mulattoes, Mammies, and Bucks: An Interpretive History of Blacks in American Films.* New York: Bantam Books, 1974.

Bond, Horace Mann. "Social and Economic Forces in Alabama Reconstruction." *Journal of Negro History* 23, no. 3 (1938): 290–348.

Bright, Steven. "Discrimination, Death, and Denial: Race and the Death Penalty." In *Machinery of Death: The Reality of America's Death Penalty Regime*, edited by David Dow and Mark Dow. New York: Routledge, 2002.

Brock, W. R. *An American Crisis: Congress and Reconstruction, 1865–1867.* London: Macmillan, 1963.

Brown, Richard. *Strain of Violence: Historical Studies of American Violence and Vigilantism.* New York: Oxford University Press, 1975.

Bryson, Norman. "The Gaze in the Expanded Field." In *Vision and Visuality*, edited by Hal Foster, 87–113. Seattle: Bay, 1988.

Burns, Walter. *The Robin Hood of El Dorado: The Saga of Joaquin Murrieta, Famous Outlaw of California's Age of Gold.* Albuquerque: University of New Mexico Press, 1999.

Butler, Judith. "Endangered/Endangering: Schematic Racism and White Paranoia." In *Reading Rodney King/Reading Urban Uprising*, edited by Robert Gooding-Williams. New York: Routledge, 1993.

Campbell, Christopher P. *Race, Myth and the News.* Thousand Oaks, CA: Sage, 1995.

Carby, Hazel. "A Strange and Bitter Crop: The Spectacle of Torture." *Open Democracy*, October 10, 2004. Available at https://www.opendemocracy.net/en/article_2149jsp/.

Carlson, James. *Primetime Law Enforcement: Crime Show Viewing and Attitudes toward the Criminal Justice System.* New York: Praeger, 1985.

Carpenter, John A. "Atrocities in the Reconstruction Period." *Journal of Negro History* 47, no. 4 (1962): 234–247.

Carr, Cynthia. "The Atrocity Exhibition." *Village Voice*, March 28, 2000.

Carrigan, William D., and Clive Webb. "The Lynching of Persons of Mexican Origin or Descent in the US, 1848 to 1928." *Journal of Social History* 37, no. 2 (2003): 411–438.

Cartwright, Lisa. *Screening the Body: Tracing Medicine's Visual Culture.* Minneapolis: University of Minnesota Press, 1998.

Center on Juvenile and Criminal Justice. "Executive Summary: America's One-Million Nonviolent Offenders." March 1999. Available at http://www.cjcj.org/uploads/cjcj/documents/americas.pdf.

Clack, Cary. "A Vow: Never Again—Images of Hate Must Compel Nation to Confront Racism." *San Antonio Express-News*, February 6, 2000.

Cole, Joshua. *The Power of Large Numbers: Population, Politics and Gender in 19th Century France*. Ithaca, NY: Cornell University Press, 2000.

Cooter, Robert. *Cultural Meaning of Popular Science: Phrenology and the Organization of Consent in Nineteenth-Century Britain*. Cambridge: Cambridge University Press, 1984.

Cornforth, Maurice. *The Theory of Knowledge*. New York: International, 1971.

Crary, Jonathan. "Modernizing Vision." In *Vision and Visuality*, edited by Hal Foster. Seattle: Bay, 1988.

Cuevas, Ofelia Ortiz. "Arresting Images: *COPS* in the 'Projects' of Race." Master's thesis, University of California, San Diego, 2000.

Curtin, Mary Ellen. *Black Prisoners and Their World, Alabama, 1865–1900*. Charlottesville: University of Virginia Press, 2000.

Davis, Angela Y. *Are Prisons Obsolete?* New York: Seven Stories, 2003.

———. "Race and Criminalization: Black Americans and the Punishment Industry." In *The House That Race Built*, edited by Wahneema Lubiano. New York: Pantheon, 1997.

Davis, Mike. *City of Quartz*. London: Verso, 1990.

———. *Prisoners of the American Dream: Politics and Economy in the History of the US Working Class*. New York: Verso, 1986.

Debord, Guy. *The Society of the Spectacle*. Detroit: Black and Red, 1977.

Dominick, Joseph. "Crime and Law Enforcement on Prime-Time Television." *Public Opinion Quarterly* 37, no. 2 (1973): 241–250.

Donzinger, Stephen. *The Real War on Crime: The Report of the National Criminal Justice Commission*. New York: Harper Collins, 1996.

Downey, Mike. "An American Holocaust." *Los Angeles Times*, February 6, 2000.

Du Bois, W.E.B. *Black Reconstruction in America, 1860–1880*. New York: Simon and Schuster, 1935.

Ellison, Ralph. *The Invisible Man*. New York: Random House, 1948.

Escobar, Edward J. *Race, Police, and the Making of a Political Identity: Mexican Americans and the Los Angeles Police Department*. Berkeley: University of California Press, 1999.

Fabian, John. *Time and the Other*. New York: Columbia University Press, 1983.

Feldman, Allen. "Commodification and Commensality in Political Violence in South Africa and Northern Ireland." *Ethnografica* 3, no. 1 (1999): 113–129.

———. *Formations of Violence: The Narrative of the Body and Political Terror in Northern Ireland*. Chicago: University of Chicago Press, 1991.

Fishman, Mark, and Gray Cavendar, eds. *Entertaining Crime: Television Reality Programs*. New York: Aldine De Gruyter, 1998.

Fiske, John. *Media Matters: Race and Gender in US Politics*. Minneapolis: University of Minnesota Press, 1994.

Fleetwood, Nicole. *Troubling Vision: Performance, Visuality and Blackness*. Chicago: University of Chicago Press, 2011.

Foley, Neil. *White Scourge: Mexicans, Blacks and Poor Whites in Texas Cotton Culture*. Berkeley: University of California Press, 1997.

Foner, Eric. "Reconstruction Revisited." *Reviews in American History* 10, no. 4 (1982): 82–100.

Foster, Hal. *Vision and Visuality*. Seattle: Bay, 1998.

Foucault, Michel. *Discipline and Punish: The Birth of the Prison*. New York: Vintage, 1977.

Fredrickson, George. "For African Americans, Justice Was Often at the End of a Rope: Lynching Photography in America." *Journal of Blacks in Higher Education* 28 (2000): 123–131.

Friedman, Lawrence. *Crime and Punishment in American History*. New York: Basic Books, 1993.

Garland, David. "Penal Excess and Surplus Meaning: Public Torture Lynchings in Twentieth-Century America." *Law and Society Review* 39, no. 4 (2005): 793–833.

Genovese, Eugene. *From Rebellion to Revolution: Afro-American Slave Revolts in the Making of the Modern World*. Baton Rouge: Louisiana State University Press, 1992.

———. *Roll Jordon Roll: The World the Slaves Made*. New York: Vintage, 1976.

Gerbner, George, and Larry Gross. "Living with Television: The Violence Profile." *Journal of Communication* 25, no. 2 (1976): 173–199.

Gilder, George. *Wealth and Poverty*. New York: Bantam Books, 1982.

Gilliam, Jr., Frank, and Shanto Iyengar. "Prime Suspects: The Influence of Local Television News on the Viewing Public." *American Journal of Political Science* 44, no. 3 (2000): 560–573.

Gilligan, James. *Violence: Reflections on a National Epidemic*. New York: Vintage, 1997.

Gilmore, Ruth. *Golden Gulag: Prisons, Surplus, Crisis, and Opposition in Globalizing California*. Berkeley: University of California Press, 2006.

Giroux, Henry A. *Counter Narratives: Cultural Studies and Critical Pedagogies in Postmodern Spaces*. New York: Routledge, 1996.

———. *Fugitive Cultures: Race, Violence and Youth*. New York: Routledge, 1996.

Gitlin, Todd. *The Whole World Is Watching: Mass Media in the Making and Unmaking of the New Left*. Berkeley: University of California Press, 1980.

Goffman, Erving. *Stigma: Notes on the Management of Spoiled Identity*. Englewood Cliffs, NJ: Prentice-Hall, 1963.

Gomes, Ralph C., and Linda F. Williams. "Race and Crime: The Role of the Media in Perpetuating Racism and Classism in America." *Urban League Review* 14, no. 1 (1992): 57–69.

Gonzalez-Day, Ken. *Lynching in the West, 1850–1935*. Durham, NC: Duke University Press, 2006.

Gordon, Avery F. *Ghostly Matters: Haunting and the Sociological Imagination*. Minneapolis: University of Minnesota Press, 1997.

———. "Globalism and the Prison Industrial Complex: An Interview with Angela Davis." *Race and Class* 40, nos. 2–3 (1998): 145–157.

Graber, Doris. *Crime News and the Public*. New York: Praeger, 1980.

Gray, Herman. "Race Relations as News." *American Behavior Scientist* 30, no. 4 (1987): 381–395.

———. *Watching Race: Television and the Struggle for "Blackness."* Minneapolis: University of Minnesota Press, 1995.

Gunning, Sandra. *Race, Rape, and Lynching: The Red Record of American Literature*. New York: Oxford University Press, 1996.

Gutierrez, Felix. *Minorities and the Media: Diversity and the End of Mass Communication*. London: Sage, 1985.

Hall, Stuart. *Policing the Crisis: Mugging, the State and Law and Order*. London: Macmillan, 1978.

——, ed. *Representations: Cultural Representations and Signifying Practices*. London: Sage, 1997.

Haraway, Donna. *Simians, Cyborgs, and Women: The Reinvention of Nature*. New York: Routledge, 1991.

——. "Teddy Bear Patriarchy: Taxidermy in the Garden of Eden, New York City 1908–1936." In *Culture/Power/History: A Reader in Contemporary Theory*, edited by Nicholas B. Dirks, Geoff Eley, and Sherry B. Ortner. Princeton, NJ: Princeton University Press, 1994.

Harris, Cheryl. "Whiteness as Property." *Harvard Law Review* 106, no. 8 (1993): 1707–1791.

Herivel, Tara, and Paul Wright. *Prison Nation: The Warehousing of America's Poor*. New York: Routledge, 2002.

Hill, Annette. *Reality TV: Audiences and Popular Factual Television*. London: Routledge, 2005.

Hill, Mike, ed. *Whiteness: A Critical Reader*. New York: New York University Press, 1997.

Holmes, Su, and Deborah Jermyn. *Understanding Reality Television*. London: Routledge, 2004.

"Homicide Report, The." *Los Angeles Times*, October 10, 2007. Available at http://www .latimes.com/news/local/crime/homicidemap.

Horseman, Reginald. *Race and Manifest Destiny: Origins of American Racial Anglo Saxonism*. Cambridge, MA: Harvard University Press, 1981.

Human Rights Watch. *Incarcerated America: Human Rights Watch Backgrounder*. April 2003. Available at https://www.hrw.org/legacy/backgrounder/usa/incarceration/us04 2903.pdf.

Hunt, Darnell. "Raced Ways of Seeing." In *Screening the Los Angeles Riots: Race Seeing and Resistance*. Cambridge: Cambridge University Press, 1995.

Illes, Chrissy, and Russell Roberts. *Visible Light: Photography and Classification in Art, Science and the Everyday*. Oxford: Museum of Modern Art, 1997.

James, A. Everett. "Images of African Americans in Southern Paintings 1840–1940." *Southern Cultures* 9, no. 2 (2003): 67–81.

James, Joy. "Erasing the Spectacle of Racialized State Violence." In *Resisting State Violence: Radicalism, Gender, and Race in US Culture*. Minneapolis: University of Minnesota Press, 1996.

Janich, Kathy. "Line Steady for Last View of Lynching Photographs." *Atlanta Journal-Constitution*, January 13, 2003.

Jay, Martin. *Downcast Eyes: The Denigration of Vision in Twentieth-Century French Thought*. Berkeley: University of California Press, 1994.

Jensen, Richard E., R. Eli Paul, and John E. Carter. *Eyewitness at Wounded Knee*. Lincoln: University of Nebraska Press, 2011.

Jewkes, Yvonne. *Media and Crime*. London: Sage, 2004.

Jhally, Sut, and Justin Lewis. *Enlightened Racism: The Bill Cosby Show, Audiences, and the Myth of the American Dream*. Boulder, CO: Westview, 1992.

Johnson, Benjamin Herber. *Revolution in Texas: How a Forgotten Rebellion and Its Bloody Suppression Turned Mexicans into Americans*. New Haven, CT: Yale University Press, 2003.

Joseph, Earl. *Eloquence and Power: The Rise of Language Standards and Standard Languages*. London: Frances Pinter, 1987.

Karp, Ivan, and Steven D. Lavine. *Exhibiting Cultures: The Poetics and Politics of Museum Display*. Washington, DC: Smithsonian Institution, 1991.

Kelley, Robin. *Yo' Mama's Disfunktional: Fighting the Culture Wars in Urban America.* Boston: Beacon, 1997.

Lane, Charles. "Editorial." *New Republic*, April 3, 1995.

Lewis, John. "Foreword." In *Without Sanctuary: Lynching Photography in America*, edited by James Allen. Santa Fe, NM: Twin Palms, 2000.

Lichtenstein, Alex. *Twice the Work of Free Labor: The Political Economy of Convict Labor in the New South.* New York: Verso, 1996.

Lidchi, Henrietta. "The Poetics and Politics of Exhibiting Other Cultures." In *Representations: Cultural Representations and Signifying Practices*, edited by Stuart Hall, 151–222. London: Sage, 1997.

Linebaugh, Peter. *The London Hanged: Crime and Civil Society in the Eighteenth Century.* Cambridge: Cambridge University Press, 1992.

Lippman, Walter. *Public Opinion.* New York: Free Press, 1922.

Lipsitz, George. *The Possessive Investment in Whiteness: How White People Profit from Identity Politics.* Philadelphia: Temple University Press, 1998.

———. "The Possessive Investment in Whiteness: Racialized Social Democracy and the 'White' Problem in American Studies." *American Quarterly* 47, no. 3 (September 1995): 369–387.

———. *Time Passages: Collective Memory and American Popular Culture.* Minneapolis: University of Minnesota Press, 1990.

Lo, Clarence Y. H., and Michael Schwartz. *Social Policy and the Conservative Agenda.* Malden, MA: Blackwell, 1998.

Lott, Eric. *Love and Theft: Black Face Minstrelsy and the American Working Class.* New York: Oxford University Press, 1993.

Louisiana Black Codes. "The Black Code of St. Landry's Parish, Louisiana." 1865.

Mancini, Matthew J. *One Dies, Get Another: Convict Leasing in the American South, 1866–1928.* Columbia: University of South Carolina Press, 1996.

———. "Race, Economics, and the Abandonment of Convict Lease." *Journal of Negro History* 63, no. 4 (1978): 339–352.

Marc, David. *Demographic Vistas: Television in American Culture.* Philadelphia: University of Pennsylvania Press, 1984.

Marcus, George E., and Michael M. Fischer. *Anthropology as Cultural Critique: An Experimental Moment in the Human Sciences.* Chicago: University of Chicago Press, 1986.

Marcus, George E., and Fred Meyers, eds. *The Traffic in Culture: Refiguring Art and Anthropology.* Berkeley: University of California Press, 1995.

Mauer, Marc. *Race to Incarcerate.* New York: New Press, 2006.

McClain, Charles. *In Search of Equality: The Chinese Struggle against Discrimination in the Nineteenth Century.* Berkeley: University of California Press, 1996.

McClintock, Anne. *Imperial Leather: Race, Gender, and Sexuality in the Colonial Contest.* New York: Routledge, 1995.

Mieder, Wolfgang. "'The Only Good Indian Is a Dead One': History and Meaning of a Proverbial Stereotype." *Journal of American Folklore* 106, no. 419 (1993): 38–60.

Miller, Ian. *The Anatomy of Disgust.* Cambridge, MA: Harvard University Press, 1998.

Miller, Jerome. *Search and Destroy: African American Males in the Criminal Justice System.* Cambridge: Cambridge University Press, 1996.

Mills, C. Wright. *The Power Elite.* New York: Oxford University Press, 1959.

Mills, Nicolaus, ed. *Culture in the Age of Money: The Legacy of the 1980s in America.* Chicago: Ivan R. Dee, 1990.

Milroy, James. *Authority in Language Prescription and Standardization.* London: Routledge, 1991.

Mirande, Alfredo. *Gringo Justice.* Notre Dame, IN: University of Notre Dame Press, 1987.

Moehringer, J. R. "Scavenger or Voyeur? Why Did James Allen Collect Pictures of Lynchings in America and Ask Us to Look at Them?" *Calgary Herald,* October 21, 2000.

Montejano, David. *Anglos and Mexicans in the Making of Texas, 1836–1986.* Austin: University of Texas Press, 1987.

Morely, David. *Television Audiences and Cultural Studies.* New York: Routledge, 1992.

Morely, Morris, and James Petras. "Wealth and Poverty in the National Economy: The Domestic Foundations of Clinton's Global Policy." In *Social Policy and the Conservative Agenda,* edited by Clarence Y. H. Lo and Michael Schwartz. New York: Blackwell, 1998.

Mulvey, Laura. *Visual and Other Pleasures.* Bloomington: Indiana University Press, 1989.

———. "Visual Pleasure and Narrative Cinema." *The Sexual Subject: A Screen Reader in Sexuality.* London: Routledge, 1992.

Newcomb, Horace. "On the Dialogic Aspects of Mass Communications." *Critical Studies in Mass Communication* 1, no. 1 (1984): 34–50.

O'Keefe, Garrett. "Public Views on Crime: Television Exposure and Media Credibility." *Annals of the International Communication Association* 8, no. 1 (1984): 514–536.

Oliver, Mary Beth, and Blake G. Armstrong. "The Color of Crime: Perceptions of Caucasians' and African Americans' Involvement in Crime." In *Entertaining Crime: Television Reality Programs,* edited by Mark Fishman and Gray Cavendar. New York: Aldine De Gruyter, 1998.

Oshinsky, David. *Worse Than Slavery: Parchman Farm and the Ordeal of Jim Crow Justice.* New York: Free Press, 1996.

Paredes, Americo. *"With a Pistol in His Hand": A Border Ballad and Its Hero.* Austin: University of Texas Press, 1958.

Parenti, Christian. *Lockdown America: Police and Prisons in the Age of Crisis.* New York: Verso, 1999.

Parvin, Paige. "Strange Fruit: Emory Takes a Hard Look at One of America's Deepest Sorrows." *Emory Magazine* (Summer 2002).

Poole, Deborah. *Vision, Race, and Modernity: A Visual Economy of the Andean Image World.* Princeton, NJ: Princeton University Press, 1997.

Reeves, Jimmie, and Richard Campbell. *Cracked Coverage: Television News, the Anti-Cocaine Crusade, and the Reagan Legacy.* Durham, NC: Duke University Press, 1994.

Rogin, Michael. *Ronald Reagan, the Movie: And Other Episodes in Political Demonology.* Berkeley: University of California Press, 1987.

Rogoff, Irit, ed. *Visual Culture: The Study of the Visual after the Cultural Turn.* Cambridge, MA: MIT Press, 2002.

Rony, Fatimah Tobing. *The Third Eye: Race Cinema and Ethnographic Spectacle.* Durham, NC: Duke University Press, 1996.

Ross, Luana. *Inventing the Savage: The Social Construction of Criminality.* Austin: University of Texas Press, 1998.

Russell, Katheryn K. *The Color of Crime: Racial Hoaxes, White Fear, Black Protectionism, Police Harassment, and Other Macroaggressions.* New York: New York University Press, 1998.

Ryan, Michael, and Doug Kellner. *Camera Politica: The Politics and Ideology of Contemporary Hollywood Film.* Bloomington: Indiana University Press, 1988.

Sahagun, Louis. "Former First Lady, Gates on Scene as SWAT Team Carries Out Drug Raid." *Los Angeles Times,* April 8, 1989.

Said, Edward. *Orientalism.* New York: Random House, 1979.

Sassen, Saskia. *Globalization and Its Discontents: Essays in the New Mobility of People and Money.* New York: New Press, 1998.

Saxton, Alexander. *The Rise and Fall of the White Republic: Class Politics and Mass Culture in Nineteenth-Century America.* New York: Verso, 1990.

Sears, David, and John McConahay. "Participation in the Los Angeles Riots: Social Problems and Ideological State Apparatuses." *Culture, Media, and Society.* London, 1981.

Sentencing Project, The. "State Rates of Incarceration by Race." May 2004.

Shah, Nayan. *Contagious Divides: Epidemics and Race in San Francisco's Chinatown.* Berkeley: University of California Press, 2001.

Shapiro, Karen A. "A New Southern Rebellion: The Battle against Convict Labor in the Tennessee Cornfields, 1871–1896." Chapel Hill: University of North Carolina Press, 1998.

Shohat, Ella, and Robert Stam. *Unthinking Eurocentrism: Multiculturalism and the Media.* New York: Routledge, 1994.

Shull, Steven A. *A Kinder, Gentler Racism? The Reagan-Bush Civil Rights Legacy.* New York: M. E. Sharpe, 1993.

Siegel, Micol. *Violence Work: State Power and the Limits of Police.* Durham, NC: Duke University Press, 2018.

Simon, David R., and D. Stanley Eitzen. *Elite Deviancy.* London: Allyn and Bacon, 1990.

Smith, Shawn Michelle. *American Archives: Gender, Race, and Class in Visual Culture.* Princeton, NJ: Princeton University Press, 1999.

Smith, Shawn Michelle, and Dora Apel. *Lynching Photographs.* Berkeley: University of California Press, 2007.

Sontag, Susan. "Regarding the Torture of Others." *New York Times,* May 23, 2004.

Stacey, Judith. "The Right Family Values." In *Social Policy and the Conservative Agenda,* edited by Clarence Y. H. Lo and Michael Schwartz. Malden, MA: Blackwell, 1998.

Stafford, Barbara Marie. *Body Criticism: Imaging the Unseen in Enlightenment Art and Medicine.* Cambridge, MA: MIT Press, 1993.

Stallybrass, Peter, and Allon White. *The Politics and Poetics of Transgression.* Ithaca, NY: Cornell University Press, 1986.

Staples, Brent. "The Perils of Growing Comfortable with Evil." *New York Times,* April 9, 2000.

Stocking, George. *Race, Culture, and Evolution: Essays in the History of Anthropology.* Chicago: University of Chicago Press, 1968.

Sturken, Marita. *Tangled Memories: The Vietnam War, the AIDS Epidemic, and the Politics of Remembering.* Berkeley: University of California Press, 1997.

Tagg, Jonathan. *The Burden of Representation: Essays on Photographies and Histories.* London: Macmillan, 1988.

Tagima-Peña, Rene, and Christine Choy. *Who Killed Vincent Chin?* Filmakers Library, 1987.

Taussig, Michael. *Shamanism, Colonialism and the Wild Man: A Study in Terror and Healing.* Chicago: University of Chicago Press, 1987.

Taylor, Lucien, ed. *Visualizing Theory: Selected Essays from V.A.R., 1990–1994.* New York: Routledge, 1994.

Taylor, P. A. *Professor Huxley on the Negro Question.* Ladies London Emancipation Society, 1864. Available at https://mathcs.clarku.edu/huxley/comm/Books/Taylor.html.

Thomas, Mary. "'Without Sanctuary' Digs Deeply into Painful Issues of Inhumanity." *Post-Gazette Art Review,* September 29, 2001.

United Nations Human Rights Committee. "In the Shadows of the War on Terror: Persistent Police Brutality and Abuse in the United States." May 2006.

U.S. Department of Justice, Bureau of Justice Statistics. "State and Federal Prison Population, 1960–1994." Washington, DC.

Valdez, Sarah. "American Abject; Exhibition; Without Sanctuary: Lynching Photography in America," *Art in America,* October 1, 2000.

Virilio, Paul. *The Vision Machine.* Bloomington: Indiana University Press, 1994.

Waldrep, Christopher. *The Many Faces of Judge Lynch.* New York: Palgrave, 2002.

Waldrep, Christopher, and Donald Nieman. *Local Matters: Race, Crime and Justice in the Nineteenth Century South.* Athens: University of Georgia Press, 2001.

Waters, Harvey F. "TV's Crime Wave Gets Real." *Newsweek,* May 15, 1989.

Weber, David, J. *Myth and the History of the Hispanic Southwest.* Albuquerque: University of New Mexico Press, 1987.

Weheliye, Alexander. *Habeas Viscus: Racializing Assemblages, Biopolitics, and Black Feminist Theories of the Human.* Durham, NC: Duke University Press, 2014.

Wells, Ida B. *On Lynching: Southern Horrors; A Red Record; Mob Rule in New Orleans.* New York: Arno, 1969.

Williams, Raymond. *Marxism and Literature.* Oxford: Oxford University Press, 1977.

"'Without Sanctuary': Artifacts of Lynching in America." National Public Radio. Available at http://www.npr.org/templates/story/story.php?storyId=1874649.

Wolcott, James. "Car 54, Where Are You?" *New Yorker,* February 8, 1993.

Wood, Amy Louise. *Lynching and Spectacle: Witnessing Racial Violence in America 1890–1940.* Chapel Hill: University of North Carolina Press, 2011.

INDEX

Ofelia Ortiz Cuevas is a transdisciplinary scholar in the Department of Chicana/o Studies at the University of California, Davis. Her work on state violence and incarceration has been published in journals including *American Quarterly* and *PUBLIC*. She is the editor of the online journal *Boom California* and a contributor to the anthology *Black and Brown Los Angeles: Beyond Conflict and Coalition*. Cuevas is the Director of Beyond the Barriers, a campus-wide initiative for formerly incarcerated and system-impacted students, faculty, and staff at the University of California, Davis.

www.ingramcontent.com/pod-product-compliance
Lightning Source LLC
Chambersburg PA
CBHW020614270326
41927CB00005B/326